2/ Auckland, 1918

Being a Partial Record of the War Service in France of the 2/Auckland Regiment during The Great War

By LIEUT.-COLONEL S. S. ALLEN
C.M.G., D.S.O.

The Naval & Military Press Ltd

Published by
The Naval & Military Press Ltd
5 Riverside, Brambleside, Bellbrook
Industrial Estate, Uckfield, East Sussex,
TN22 1QQ England
Tel: +44 (0) 1825 749494
Fax: +44 (0) 1825 765701
www.naval-military-press.com
www.military-genealogy.com
www.militarymaproom.com

In reprinting in facsimile from the original, any imperfections are inevitably reproduced and the quality may fall short of modern type and cartographic standards.

CONTENTS

Chapter	Page
I—2/ Auckland	5
II—The New Zealand Division	9
III—The Higher Command	13
IV—Ypres and Zuytpeene	17
V—La Signy Farm	25
VI—The Purple Line	49
VII—Trench Warfare	57
VIII—At Rest and More Trench Warfare	73
IX—Grevillers	87
X—Bancourt	108
XI—Reorganisation and Rest	114
XII—Welsh Ridge	119
XIII—Crêvecœur	135
XIV—Fontaine-au-Tertre Farm	151
XV—Resting at Fontaine and Solesmes	162
XVI—Le Quesnoy	169
XVII—The Armistice	172
XVIII—The March Through Belgium	176
XIX—The End	186

APPENDIX

THE following table gives the numbers of all ranks who were on the roll of the 2nd Battalion Auckland Regiment during its whole existence, as well as the numbers who were killed:—

On the Battalion roll—

Officers	Other Ranks	Total
188	4073	4261

Killed, died of wounds and missing—

Officers	Other Ranks	Total
46	694	740

The proportion of killed was thus approximately one in every six who served with the Battalion. The proportion of officers killed was approximately one in four.

CHAPTER I

2/ AUCKLAND

THE 2nd Battalion, Auckland Regiment, has done more fighting in France than any other battalion in the New Zealand Division. This may seem a bold statement but it is amply corroborated by the facts, as the following brief record of the actions in which it has been engaged will show beyond possibility of dispute.

Battle of the Somme, 1916.—2/ Auckland and 2/ Otago were the first New Zealand battalions to go over the top in France. This was in the battle of the 15th September —the first occasion on which tanks were used—which resulted in the most signal British victory up to that time in the war. In the fighting which followed that battle, 2/ Auckland was engaged again in operations round the Flers and Gird trenches.

Fleurbaix, 1917.—The whole battalion was employed on a raid, the only one on so large a scale ever tried by the N.Z.

2/ AUCKLAND

Division. The raid was quite successful, and its result was the capture of a number of prisoners and acquirement of much valuable information.

Messines, 1917.—The battalion held the whole Divisional front during the five days' preliminary bombardment, and after this trying experience was one of the two battalions to go furthest and establish the most advanced posts in the attack on the 7th June.

Ypres, 1917.—On the 4th October, in the attack on Gravenstafel Ridge, 2/ Auckland and 2/ Wellington were the battalions detailed to capture the final objective on the 1st Brigade front.

The exploits of the battalion in 1918 form the subject of this book, but it is convenient to summarise them now.

27th March.—The battalion was in support to 1/ Auckland and 2/ N.Z.R.B. in the advance from Hedauville to a position in front of Mailly Maillet, and relieved the 2/ N.Z.R.B. early the following morning.

30th March.—2/ Auckland, with assistance on the right and left from 1/ Wellington and

2/ AUCKLAND

4/N.Z.R.B., fought the memorable little battle of La Signy Farm.

24th August.—In the fighting round Bapaume 2/ Auckland was the first battalion of the 1st Brigade to be engaged, and took the village of Grevillers.

30th August and subsequent days.—The battalion took Bancourt and the ridge to the east of that village in one of the hardest battles of the 1918 offensive.

29th September.—Battle of Welsh Ridge, 1/ Auckland and 2/ Auckland were on the left of the Brigade, and penetrated furthest beyond the German positions.

30th September.—2/ Auckland seized and held the bridge over the Escaut River at Crêvecœur.

10th October.—2/ Auckland on the left and 2/ Wellington on the right advanced to the Selle River, the latter crossing it in front of Briastre.

4th November.—Battle of Le Quesnoy. In the final battle of the war, 2/ Auckland was in Brigade Reserve, for the only occasion in which the Brigade has been engaged, and con-

2/ AUCKLAND

sequently took no prominent part in the battle. With such a record of fighting it is no wonder that the battalion has a high opinion of itself, and it is right that its history should be recorded in some detail. To describe the period of 1916 and 1917 with its monotonous trench warfare, broken only by two or three battles, would not be of such general interest, but the changing scenes of 1918 are of a more absorbing nature. Before commencing the narrative, however, a preliminary chapter on the composition and earlier history of the battalion is necessary.

CHAPTER II

THE NEW ZEALAND DIVISION

THE original New Zealand Expeditionary Force, the N.Z.E.F., as it will be more convenient to call it, was dispatched from New Zealand in October, 1914. As far as the infantry were concerned, it consisted of the Auckland, Canterbury, Otago and Wellington Regiments, each of one battalion only, drawn from the four military districts into which the Dominion of New Zealand is divided. For some years past there has been a system of compulsory service in the territorial forces in New Zealand, and in the Auckland District there are four infantry territorial Regiments, the 3rd (Auckland) Regiment, 6th (Hauraki) Regiment, 15th (North Auckland) Regiment, and 16th (Waikato) Regiment. Each of these Regiments, or rather the areas from which they are drawn, provided a company of the original Auckland Battalion; and the four companies of that battalion were named after these four regiments—the 3rd (Auckland)

THE NEW ZEALAND DIVISION

Company, 6th (Hauraki) Company, 15th (North Auckland) Company, and 16th (Waikato) Company respectively. Each of these companies also wore the badge of the territorial Regiment after which it was named, so that the badges in the battalion were company badges and not regimental. The same system was adhered to in the other battalions of the N.Z.E.F., and was preserved when second battalions of the regiments in the original force were formed, and the nomenclature has always proved somewhat puzzling to outsiders.

After the evacuation of the Gallipoli Peninsula in December, 1915, the N.Z.E.F. returned to Egypt. It was decided to expand it considerably, the mounted brigade was left in Egypt, and the remainder of the force became a Division under the command of Major-General Russell—now Sir A. H. Russell, K.C.B., K.C.M.G. Each battalion in the original brigade was broken into two, and the four new battalions thus formed, 2/ Auckland, 2/ Canterbury, 2/ Otago and 2/ Wellington became the 2nd Brigade, commanded by Brigadier-General Braithwaite. The third Brigade neces-

THE NEW ZEALAND DIVISION

sary to complete the Division, the 3rd New Zealand Rifle Brigade, was formed brand new from New Zealand.

The 2nd Brigade was formed on the 1st March, 1916, and 2/ Auckland was commanded from that date till June, 1916, by Lieut.-Col. W. W. Alderman, who belongs to the Australian Staff Corps, and sailed from New Zealand with the original N.Z.E.F. The battalion came to France with the New Zealand Division in April, 1916, and in June, 1916, Lieut.-Col. Alderman was succeeded in the command of the battalion by Lieut.-Col. J. W. H. Brown, afterwards Brigadier-General, who was unfortunately killed while commanding the 1st Brigade at Messines in June, 1917. General Brown was perhaps the finest soldier who left New Zealand, and his untimely death was nowhere regretted more than in his old battalion. In January, 1917, on the promotion of Lieut.-Col. Brown, I was promoted Lieut.-Col., and commanded the battalion from that time. I had previously been 2nd in command, first under Lieut.-Col. Alderman and later under Lieut.-Col. Brown, so that I

THE NEW ZEALAND DIVISION

have belonged to 2/ Auckland throughout its whole existence.

In January, 1917, the 1st and 2nd Brigades were reorganised, 2/ Auckland and 2/ Wellington going to the 1st Brigade from the 2nd, and 1/ Canterbury and 1/ Otago to the 2nd Brigade from the 1st. From that time onward the four battalions of the 1st Brigade have been 1 and 2/ Auckland and 1 and 2/ Wellington. The 1st Brigade was then commanded by Brigadier-General Brown, and from his death in June, 1917, it has been commanded almost without a break by Brigadier-General Melvill.

CHAPTER III

THE HIGHER COMMAND

THE New Zealand Division has always been fortunate in the men who have held the higher commands in it. From the formation of the Division in 1915 it has been commanded by Sir A. H. Russell. An officer in the Regular Army in early life, he had been farming in New Zealand for many years before the war started in 1914. During his life in New Zealand he had been keenly interested in all military questions, and held the rank of Colonel in the territorial forces. In the original N.Z.E.F. he commanded the Brigade of Mounted Rifles, which he left to assume command of the Division in 1915. The Division owes much of its reputation to his ability in handling it, as well as to his remarkable skill and judgment in administration. He has always held the entire confidence of all who have served under him, and there is not an officer or man in the Division who would hesitate to carry out anything he ordered, the

THE HIGHER COMMAND

General being, in their opinion, one of the ablest soldiers in France.

Brigadier-General Melvill, commanding the 1st Brigade, is another former Regular. He had left the Regular Army and was farming in New Zealand when the territorial force came into existence in 1911. He then entered the New Zealand Staff Corps, and in 1914 was at the Staff College at Camberley. When the war started he went to France with his old regiment, and saw much heavy fighting in the autumn of 1914. He was wounded, and on his recovery came to Gallipoli to join the N.Z.E.F., with which he served for about a month before the evacuation. When the New Zealand Division was formed, he was first Brigade-Major of the 2nd Brigade, and afterwards commanded the 4th Battalion of the N.Z. Rifle Brigade, till, on the death of General Brown he was promoted Brigadier-General, and took command of the 1st Brigade. The principal achievements of the 1st Brigade will always be associated with his name. He hardly ever made a mistake; and while his cheerful personality made him popular with all

THE HIGHER COMMAND

ranks, his tactful suggestions of possible lines of action were most helpful to his Commanding Officers. As one of the Commanding Officers myself, I can say that on all the occasions on which my battalion fought a successful action, that success was due to the precision with which General Melvill had foreseen and provided against the difficulties which might arise. If I take credit to myself in this book for executing any action, it must be remembered that I was really only carrying it out as closely as possible along the lines he had suggested. General Melvill never interfered with a battalion commander more than he could help, and never gave more definite orders than were necessary, but he was always ready to advise, and his advice always proved sound. Altogether, with the possible exception of General Brown, it is hard to imagine a finer type of Brigadier under whom to work.

In 1918, the Brigade Major of the 1st Brigade was Major W. I. K. Jennings, another survivor of the original N.Z.E.F., and one of the younger members of the New Zealand Staff Corps. The Staff Corps has not produced

THE HIGHER COMMAND

many successful officers, but Major Jennings, like the Brigadier himself, was one of the exceptions to this rule. The Staff Captain during nearly all the period covered by this book was Captain Holderness. The job of Staff Captain is a very thankless one, and consists of dealing with work no one wants to do. It requires industry, tact and perseverance, all of which qualities Captain Holderness possessed.

CHAPTER IV

YPRES AND ZUYTPEENE

I WAS somewhat severely wounded at the battle of Gravenstafel on the 4th October, 1917, and spent all the winter in hospital, returning to resume command of the battalion towards the end of February, 1918. The Division spent the winter in the Ypres sector, and its main occupation had been digging, in view of a possible German attack in the spring. Every day when the battalion was not actually in the trenches large working parties were engaged in digging strong points, building concrete shelters and erecting barb wire. The work was hard, and involved long distances to be marched to and fro every day. The efficiency of the battalion had been somewhat neglected, and when I rejoined it on the 24th February, 1918, I was rather struck with the poor appearance of the men. Clothing had not received much attention, and one constant source of trouble which had been eradicated during the previous summer had appeared

YPRES AND ZUYTPEENE

again—this was the wearing of clothing other than the regulation pattern. It should be explained that the New Zealand soldier is firmly convinced that he looks better in riding breeches than in the trousers which are issued to him, and many buy a pair of breeches when they go on leave. If their appearance on parade in breeches is not firmly checked they ultimately discard the trousers altogether. This had been overlooked during the winter; and when on my return the battalion had to appear in regulation dress, the rags they produced to wear were a sorry sight indeed. This and other irregularities took a little while to overcome.

On the 24th February, the battalion was living at West Farm Camp near the Menin Road, east of Ypres. The camp consisted of a number of scattered Nissen huts, which are semi-cylindrical structures of corrugated iron, each holding about twenty men. Each hut was surrounded by earth walls as a protection against bombs dropped from aircraft. These huts are more comfortable than dugouts, as they are dry and airy, but that is about all,

YPRES AND ZUYTPEENE

and in cold weather with the scanty fuel allowance it is hard to keep any semblance of warmth in them. We contrived to keep them habitable, however, by sending limbers forward to collect firewood in the devastated area near Château Wood, a somewhat risky proceeding owing to enemy shell fire. On the 8th March the battalion moved to Ottawa Camp, west of Ypres, and on the 10th went on by motor lorry to Zuytpeene for what was intended to be a month of rest and training.

Zuytpeene is a typical little Flemish village, built round a square with the church in the middle of it. There was room in the village itself for battalion headquarters, and the companies were billeted in farms within easy distance. Everyone enjoyed the change from the strenuous work at Ypres; the weather was remarkably warm for the season, and the billets as comfortable as could reasonably be expected. Training was carried on in the mornings for four hours a day, and platoon, company and battalion football competitions were begun. We did not see much of the other battalions, as the Brigade was scattered, and

YPRES AND ZUYTPEENE

distances between them were considerable. We were about four miles from Brigade Headquarters at Staple. General Russell inspected the battalion on a day of pouring rain, and did not seem greatly impressed with our appearance, though the ragged appearance the battalion had presented a fortnight before was gradually being eliminated and the boots and clothing brought up to a better standard. On the 17th General Russell did a tactical exercise with the Commanding Officers of the Brigade, which was remarkable for its accurate forecast of the breakdown on the Lys front, which actually occurred three weeks later, the underlying idea being that our line south of Armentieres had been broken and that Hazebrouck was threatened.

On the 21st March, we marched sixteen miles through St. Omer to Houlle, where we intended to spend several days on the range for training in musketry and Lewis gun firing. On that day, however, came the great German attack on the 3rd and 5th Armies, and on the following morning we were hurried back in motor lorries to our old billets at Zuytpeene,

YPRES AND ZUYTPEENE

where we remained to the 24th, to enter on what proved to be the most exciting period of the battalion's existence. Before continuing the narrative further, it will be best to describe a little of the organisation of the battalion of that time.

At Zuytpeene, Major Shepherd had joined the battalion and for two or three weeks, until he afterwards was posted to the Rifle Brigade, he acted as second in command. He had seen a great deal of fighting, having left New Zealand with the Main Body as a platoon commander in the Canterbury Regiment. He was a most pleasant man to work with and I was genuinely sorry when he was afterwards moved from us. The companies were commanded as follows—

3rd Company, O.C., Capt. Paterson.
 Second in command, Capt. Derrom.
6th Company, O.C., Lieut. (temp.-Capt.) Moncrief.
 Second in command, Lieut. Newton.
15th Company, O.C., Capt. McArthur.
 Second in command, Capt. Napier.

YPRES AND ZUYTPEENE

16th Company, O.C., Capt. McFarland.
  Second in command, Lieut. (temp.-Capt.) C. H. S. Johnston.

At Zuytpeene, Lieut. Porritt had been acting as Adjutant, but I was doubtful about his health standing the hard work which duty in that capacity involves, so I gave him back his former work as Lewis Gun Officer and appointed Lieut. (afterwards acting Captain) Tuck as Adjutant. This very capable officer had for some time been Quartermaster, and was replaced in that duty by Lieut. Stewart. Other specialist officers with the battalion were Lieut. Ruddock, Transport officer, and Lieut. Eccles, Intelligence officer. The Padre, the Rev. C. J. H. Dobson was a very old identity with the battalion and the Medical officer was Capt. Harpur, who had come to the battalion recently.

Before leaving Zuytpeene we got no very definite news as to the extent of the German successes, but rumours as usual floated round which magnified or reduced it according to the taste of the individuals who spread them. On the whole we thought the attack was held

YPRES AND ZUYTPEENE

and were hardly prepared for what we afterwards found to be the case, but we fully expected to be in the thick of it soon.

On the last day before we left Zuytpeene, a very interesting event took place. This was a conference called together by General Russell at St. Marie Capelle to consider the advisability of starting an educational scheme in the Division which should operate during the winter months, and any period of demobilisation. Three representatives from each infantry Brigade and three from other units in the Division were summoned, not quite all of whom were present at the meeting. I was one of the three from the 1st Brigade. We decided that it was possible and desirable to start a system of education and laid down the outline of a constitution for it, and defined its objects. At a later date General Russell appointed a Board of Governors, five in number of whom I was one, to manage the scheme, and the ultimate result of it was that the machinery for education in the Division was ready to be put in operation when the armistice finally came. It is hardly necessary here to

YPRES AND ZUYTPEENE

speak of the value of the scheme, the credit for the conception of which in the Division entirely belongs to General Russell. I believe the Canadians were the only troops who were before us in preparing anything of the sort.

I should mention, before passing on to our journey from Zuytpeene, that the Second Army Signalling School was then situated at that place. Through the courtesy of the school commandant I was able, when we went away, to leave seven of my battalion signallers unofficially at the school. All seven rejoined the battalion next month with Assistant Instructor's certificates, the highest that could be obtained. This was the means of our having through the rest of the year the best trained signalling section in the Division, a matter of the greatest value in the active warfare we went through.

CHAPTER V

LA SIGNY FARM

WE received our orders to move, and left Zuytpeene on Sunday, the 24th March. The morning was spent in packing and getting ready for the move by storing our surplus baggage in a room I hired in the village, so that we could travel without more gear than was necessary. Church parade was at 2p.m., and was unusually impressive from the thought that must have been present with everyone that to many it would be their last. In the evening the battalion marched two miles to Cassel station, where we entrained. It was fortunate the distance was no greater, for the battalion had been paid the day previously, and there was a distinct exhilaration in the ranks, especially in the band, whose strains of music on the march were uncertain and wavering. The train was of the usual strategical type, familiar in France, consisting of flat open trucks for the transport vehicles, a passenger carriage for officers, and goods

LA SIGNY FARM

wagons marked with the well-known inscription " Hommes 40, Chevaux en long 8," into which were packed the men and horses. A tactical train differs from the above in that it provides accommodation for men only, while the transport travels by road, and it is then only used for shorter distances. One train accommodates a battalion.

We left Cassel station at 11 p.m., and after the usual uncomfortable night on a train arrived at Hangest-sur-Somme at 10 a.m. next morning. Our original destination was Corbie, but owing to the rapid progress of the German advance it was changed at the last moment. On our arrival we detrained, and the next problem was what to do. We were met by Major W. L. Robinson, the D.A.Q.M.G. of the Division, who could give no definite information as to where the Brigade was and where we had to go, except that it was in the general direction of Pont Noyelles, the other side of Amiens, and that sixty motor lorries were on the road taking battalions forward as they arrived. He suggested waiting on the spot for them, but I am glad I did not, or

LA SIGNY FARM

I might have been waiting still. The lorries had just gone off with 1st Auckland, who had arrived in the train before ours, and I calculated that they could hardly get back that day. There was a Major on the Army Staff at the station who was most helpful. From him I gathered the extent of the breakdown of the 5th Army under the German attack, that the news was now a little more hopeful, but that it was imperative that no time should be lost by anyone in reaching the front. I therefore decided to march forward at once, hoping that the lorries would meet us on the road during the afternoon. We had a lorry load of baggage on the train with us, mostly blankets, which I left at Hangest with our Brass Band to guard them, and arranged with the R.T.O. for the band to be rationed there. It was a fine clear morning, with a cold east wind blowing as we marched away from Hangest, and at the first sheltered spot on the road we halted for an hour for lunch. During the afternoon we marched through Picquigny, a familiar place to many of us because we had been billeted there for four days in 1916 on our way to the battle of the Somme, and I halted there for half an hour to get in touch with the motor transport, who had their headquarters there. Before dusk we reached the village of Breilly, where I found a good place to bivouac for the night just off the road. A good billet for Headquarters was discovered in a house by the road, where there were five spare beds, and we were able to buy eggs and make a most luxurious tea. Here, too, we got a room to store the men's packs and everything else that could be left behind, so that the journey was continued afterwards in fighting kit—every man and officer having with him just the clothes he stood up in without greatcoat or any other superfluous gear. Between Picquigny and Breilly we met the first of the refugees coming from Amiens. It was a pitiful sight. The more fortunate had carts piled high with their household goods, while the family walked alongside; others struggled along the road on foot carrying with them all they could save from their homes. All were wearing their best clothes, as the easiest means of carrying them. It turned out a bitterly cold frosty

LA SIGNY FARM

night, and those were lucky indeed who found any shelter.

Soon after midnight, while I was enjoying a splendid sleep in a comfortable bed at Breilly, a runner woke me up to say the motor lorries were outside. I went outside to find them there, but while we slept the 4th Battalion of the N.Z. Rifle Brigade had come up and got into the lorries, which were ready to move off. Somehow I convinced the officer in command of the lorry convoy and Lieut.-Col. Beere, of the 4th N.Z.R.B., that we had the prior claim, and not without grumbling a little the Rifle Brigade vacated the lorries and we got into them. By 1.30 in the morning we were on the move. We passed through Amiens in the early hours of the morning and reached Pont Noyelles at 5.30 a.m. There we found Major Robinson again, and received orders from him to march on to Hedauville, a distance of 12 miles, where the Division was being assembled. It was still dark when we moved off along the main road towards Albert, from which we presently turned off to the left, and after a halt for an hour for breakfast,

LA SIGNY FARM

reached Hedauville about midday. The roads were curiously deserted. Hardly a soul was to be seen, and the only troops we met were a battery of 6-inch howitzers which were blocking the road and delayed us some time in one of the villages. As we reached Hedauville we could see occasional shells bursting some distance to the east, and one or two of our own heavier guns in action, and just before we entered the village we passed some tanks of the new " whippet " variety, which no one in the battalion had seen before.

The whole division, less about two battalions which had not yet come up, was concentrated in a field on the eastern edge of Hedauville, in the bottom of a long valley leading up towards Mailly-Maillet. As soon as we arrived the men settled down for lunch, and I was sent for to a conference of Commanding Officers with the Brigadier, who explained the situation. As two battalions had not arrived, the Brigades were reorganised for the occasion, and our Brigade consisted of 1/ Auckland, 2/ N.Z.R.B., and 2/ Auckland, with 1/ Wellington, who were supposed to be

LA SIGNY FARM

not far behind, forming a sort of sketchy reserve in the background. It appeared that a gap existed between the 42nd Division, on the right of the 4th Corps and the 5th Corps, and the enemy were pushing into this gap through Serre towards the high ground about Colincamps and Mailly-Mallet. The 42nd Division were last reported on the line Puisieux-Bucquoy, but the situation was a little indefinite. The New Zealand Division was to push forward and close the gap, with the 2nd Brigade on the right and our Brigade on the left, to occupy the general line Beaumont-Hamel-Serre-Puisieux, the objective of our Brigade being Serre-Puisieux. The attack was to be launched forthwith, and our Brigade was to advance with 1/ Auckland on the right, 2/ N.Z.R.B. on the left, and 2/ Auckland in support astride of the road from Hedauville through Mailly-Maillet to Serre. At that time 1/ N.Z.R.B. was holding an outpost line covering Mailly-Mallet to protect the advance. My own battalion was tired after the march, and no doubt the others were not much less so, but everyone seemed in the highest spirits. I

LA SIGNY FARM

suppose all the Commanding Officers were like myself, not so well used to acting quickly on our orders as we became later in the year; we had had no previous experience of open warfare, and that is probably the reason for much of the delay in attacking which ensued. The 2nd Brigade were moving first, and they seemed the worst offenders. Finally 2/Auckland got on the move about half-past three in the afternoon, and moved forward up the long valley till we ran into 1/Auckland halted on the western edge of Mailly-Maillet. I was too lame to do any walking, and rode forward on a bicycle to reconnoitre the country for myself. I passed through the village and went along the Serre road till I came across a dead horse that looked rather ominous, and turned back to the village, where I saw the Brigadier and General Russell. The attack developed shortly after, and my battalion passed through the village and took up a position on its eastern edge. Brigade Headquarters was then in a house in the middle of the village, and remained there while we were in the sector. All we saw of the battle that

LA SIGNY FARM

evening were the prisoners coming back. As far as it went the fight was a success. The second Brigade went through Auchonvillers, but failed to reach Beaumont Hamel; our Brigade passed the sugar factory about two miles east of Mailly-Maillet, but failed to reach Serre, and took up a position astride of the main road just east of the hedges of La Signy Farm. The 3rd Brigade, with which 2/ Wellington was then working, were brought round on our left, drove the German patrols out of Colincamps, and linked us up with a Brigade of the 4th Australian Division, which had come down from the north and occupied Hébuterne; and they again were in touch with the 42nd Division, which had fallen back further than was at first supposed, and had its right at Gommecourt. On our Brigade front we were just short of the old 1916 front line with its maze of trenches, which the Germans now held, but we had a firm footing in the communication trenches leading up to them.

A description of the ground now will make the narrative clearer. The ground we were on is one of the watersheds of France, high

LA SIGNY FARM

rolling chalk country in which the Ancre and other small tributaries of the Somme take their rise, their valleys running south and west. Within two or three miles to the north-east the valleys begin to run in the opposite direction towards the Scarpe and the Escaut. One branch of the Ancre takes its rise near Puisieux, and in the triangle between Puisieux, Hébuterne and La Signy Farm there is a large basin, the eastern rim of which runs from La Signy Farm to Hébuterne, and this rim being slightly higher than the ground a little further west, intercepts the view in both directions. From this rim there is a very extensive view to the south-east across the basin to Puisieux and over the ground still farther east as far as Achiet-le-grand and Grevillers. The southern edge of the basin is formed by a long spur just south of La Signy Farm running out to Serre, and along the top of the spur is the road from Mailly-Maillet to Serre. The highest ground in the neighbourhood is the ridge from which this spur springs running south-east from Colincamps, and from the top of this ridge at Colincamps there is a magnificent

LA SIGNY FARM

view in all directions. All the villages are partially concealed by the trees which grow in and around them, as well as the orchards, of which there are many; but except around the villages and in two or three well-defined woods there are no trees in the country at all, and few hedges or fences of any sort. Round the enclosure of La Signy Farm there was a hedge, and the hedge to the west of the farm was prolonged both ways and ran along the rim of the basin I have described. Whoever possessed that hedge got observation over the basin at Puisieux, but from any point west of the hedge there was no view into the basin at all. The value of its possession may be judged from the fact that in 1916 all the Observation Posts of our artillery on this sector were situated in and about it.

On the evening of the 26th our attack had stopped short by two or three hundred yards of the hedge. To the right 1/ Auckland were south of the Serre road, with 2/ N.Z.R.B. on the left to the north of it. At 10 o'clock, when we thought we had settled for the night, we were moved forward to the Apple Tree on

LA SIGNY FARM

the Serre road, about half-way between Mailly-Maillet and our front line. It was a bitterly cold night, freezing hard, and none of us had even a greatcoat to put on, and many of the men, though tired out with the journey, walked up and down most of the night to keep warm. Probably I should have done so myself, but being too lame to walk, lay down and fell asleep instead. At 1 o'clock in the morning orders came to relieve the 2/ N.Z.R.B. by 5 a.m., and I went forward with the Company Commanders to find out Colonel Pow's dispositions, sending them back again to bring up their companies, and finally completing the relief about half-past four. The 2/ N.Z.R.B., of course, went back to their own Brigade.

Colonel Pow had been living under a sheet of iron in the trench, but at daylight in the morning I moved my Headquarters to an old dug-out in the road from the sugar factory to Colincamps. This dug-out was a relic of the 1916 fighting, and was, in fact, a buried Nissen hut, and into it by a very tight squeeze I got my headquarters officers, Tuck, Porritt and Eccles—battalion signallers, runners, and one

LA SIGNY FARM

or two stray details, as well as Major Shepherd and myself. As mentioned before, the 1st Brigade was astride the Mailly-Maillet-Serre road, which ran east and west through our front, with 1/ Auckland on the right to the south of it, while 2/ Auckland was now to the north of it. On our side of this road some four hundred yards back from our front line stood the ruins of a large sugar factory, in a dug-out behind which we put our R.A.P. (Regimental Aid Post), where the Doctor lived with his staff. Just east of the sugar factory a road left the main road at right angles, and ran parallel to our front, and it was in a dug-out in the side of this road that my Headquarters were now situated. After passing Headquarters the road turned away to Colincamps on our left rear, and at the bend in the road another road turned off to the left front to the hedge at La Signy Farm and on along the rim of the basin to Hébuterne. Behind Headquarters across the road was a very large dump (Euston dump) of 18-pounder cartridges, which the Germans had set fire to the previous day, and after burning all night

LA SIGNY FARM

it was still smouldering. Besides the ammunition, there was on the dump a great quantity of railway iron and sleepers, timber, shovels, and half-a-million sandbags. Most valuable of all to us in that cold weather were some bales of thick gas blanket that we subsequently found there. To the left of Headquarters, between us and the Hébuterne road, was a salvage dump of Stokes mortar and medium trench mortar (plum pudding) bombs, as well as large quantities of Mills bombs, which, unfortunately for us, were not detonated. To the right between us and the Serre road were three old communication trenches leading towards the hedge, in which trenches I placed the 15th Company. To the left in another communication trench (Southern Avenue), and in Railway Avenue on the other side of the Hébuterne road was the 16th Coy. The 6th Coy. was in reserve in Railway Avenue farther back towards Colincamps and were in more or less sketchy touch with 2/Wellington who came in on our left, and the 3rd Coy. were also in reserve behind Headquarters in some old dug-outs by Euston

LA SIGNY FARM

Dump. The trenches were ruinous after eighteen months of decay and great caution was needed in going along them to avoid machine gun and rifle bullets which swept them from time to time; there were no cross trenches joining them together so that parts were isolated and it was difficult and dangerous to get from one to the other. By the dump the Colincamps road was slightly sunken and so sheltered from enemy fire, but unfortunately for us a 2/ Wellington machine gunner made it his special target and gave everyone using it a very lively time till 4.30 in the afternoon when apparently he discovered his mistake, and ceased fire.

Our position was difficult, and on our right particularly precarious, as the posts on that flank could not support each other. The Huns realised our position and made repeated bombing attacks down the saps against the 15th Coy., which we beat off with difficulty after considerable loss. On more than one occasion it was necessary for Lieut. Hanna's platoon of the 3rd Coy. to give assistance to the posts in the sap on my immediate right. In one trench

LA SIGNY FARM

Lieut. Harrison of the 15th Coy. made a very good fight, and in beating off one of the attacks had a single combat and shot a Hun, who to judge from Harrison's account was a giant of unusual size and prodigious ferocity. About mid-day on the 28th after half an hours preparation of artillery and machine gun fire the enemy made a determined attack against ourselves and the battalion on our left, leaving his trenches in large numbers and coming across country. That this attack completely failed, is mainly due to the Lewis gunners of the 16th Coy. That night as the 15th Coy. had lost heavily I relieved them with the 6th, the two Coys. changing places. Among the 15th Coy. casualties was Capt. McArthur, who died of wounds a few days later; an officer who had left New Zealand with me, I had a great admiration for his dash and courage and greatly regretted his sad loss at so early an age. The 15th Coy. was then commanded by Capt. Napier, and Lieut. (later temporary Capt.) Harrison became second in command.

Next morning (the 29th) General Melvill came to see us. It was clear that we must im-

LA SIGNY FARM

prove our position so as to avoid the heavy casualties we were sustaining, and the two alternatives were to take the line which the Huns held or to dig a new one where we were. I preferred the former, and it was decided on provisionally. For an attack, I thought the three factors to consider were the weather, the fatigue of the men, and an adequate supply of Stokes mortars. I did not want to attack on a wet day which would impede movement in the trenches, and the men were hourly getting more tired, but on the other hand the provision of plenty of Stokes mortars seemed to me essential in attacking so strong a position. The General agreed with me and made most helpful suggestions about the method of attack and an artillery barrage. Later on he rang me up and it was settled to attack next day at 2 p.m. I went on a bicycle to Mailly Maillet to arrange final details and get from the General the artillery arrangements for the barrage. A conference with the Company commanders after I returned and all was ready.

The idea was to drive the Hun out of the hedge and hold it as our front line. On our

TRENCH WARFARE

right 1/Wellington who had relieved 1/Auckland were to co-operate by swinging their left forward in touch with our right. On our left was now the 4/ N.Z.R.B., who were left free to act as they saw opportunity. If our attack was succesful our left flank would be in the air, but it was thought by General Melvill, correctly as the event showed, that the portions of the hedge on our left would be untenable by the Hun if we were successful, and that the enemy would be pinched out of the corner between ourselves and the 4/ N.Z.R.B. On our front the 3rd Company was to attack and take the fence from the Serre road to Southern Avenue, the 6th Company assisting by clearing the communication trenches with bombing parties; the 16th Company to attack on the left from Southern Avenue inclusive. Most difficulty was expected on the right and five Stokes mortars were placed to cover that part, with one covering the left. The eighteen-pounder barrage was to open 100 yards from the hedge, move by lifts of 50 yards a minute to the hedge, and then lift to 200 yards beyond it. Very valuable reconnaissance work was

TRENCH WARFARE

done on the left by Capt. McFarland during the night, in locating enemy machine guns. The attacking Companies had to assemble in the communication trenches; the 16th in Southern Avenue, and the 3rd with the 6th behind them in the other three trenches on the right, and the attack was, of course, complicated by the fact that these trenches were not parallel with the enemy front, but ran straight towards it, so that on the barrage opening the attacking parties had to leave the trenches and extend under fire for the advance—a very trying operation.

The 29th March had been a fairly quiet day, and the morning of the 30th, the day of the attack, was still more peaceful. Our guns did some desultory registration on the hedge. The day, Easter Saturday, after a cold night was warm and fine, though a shower came on just after the attack started. Before 2 p.m. everything was ready, and I posted myself with Capt. Tuck under a hawthorn bush near Headquarters, where we could watch the ground over which the 16th would attack. We were joined by Capt. Morgan, an excellent

LA SIGNY FARM

officer who commanded the Stokes mortars. At 2 p.m. the barrage opened. It was beautifully accurate, as was also the fire of the mortars. I saw the 16th Coy. leave the trench, extend to the left, and advance steadily to the hedge. The whole movement was done as if on parade. As they moved forward I watched carefully to see if any one fell out, but apparently there was hardly a casualty, and I saw them reach the fence and drop into the trench that ran along it, and within eight minutes of the attack starting was able to telephone to Brigade that on my left we had reached our objective. Meanwhile, of course, the German artillery had opened fire, but they did us little damage, though as their barrage line apparently was the road past headquarters it was very unpleasant. On the right there was heavy machine-gun fire, but we could not see how the 3rd Coy. progressed. A few prisoners began to drift back from the hedge, and I thought the whole attack had succeeded when about 2.15 I got a most illegible message from Capt. McFarland asking for assistance, and saying a strong point at

LA SIGNY FARM

the end of Southern Avenue was still holding out. This point was important, because it was at the junction of the 3rd and 16th Companies' objectives, and one platoon of the 16th Coy. had been assigned for its capture. I sent for a platoon of the 15th Coy., which was in readiness to reinforce up Southern Avenue, and immediately went up there myself with Capt. Morgan, who volunteered to accompany me. As we got near the hedge we came on what I consider the most ghastly sight I have ever seen in all my experience in the war, fourteen dead or dying men of one platoon of the 16th Coy., all of whom had been shot in the head as they tried to climb out of the trench, and were now lying in heaps at the bottom of it. Capt. McFarland himself was standing in the trench, with a nasty head wound. It appeared the Huns were still holding a short length of the hedge and trench along it, at a point where the trench was crossed by a large culvert named Waterloo Bridge. Here they had several machine guns which had cut up this platoon of the 16th Coy. Prompt action was needed, and a Stokes mor-

LA SIGNY FARM

tar was the best weapon to dislodge them with, and after getting one of them into action the enemy post promptly surrendered. This brought the 16th Coy. into touch with the 3rd on their right. I went back to headquarters, seeing with pleasure a large number of prisoners going back from the hedge. These we had difficulty in handling, as no men could be spared for escort, but we started them back on the road to Mailly Maillet, and they were only too glad to get away from their own shells falling round our headquarters. Word came back about 3 o'clock that the 3rd Company had gained their objective, but were not in touch with 1st Wellington on their right. The Padre and I went up to see what was the matter, and found another machine gun post was holding out on the extreme right by the Serre Road, but this was reduced by a bombing party while we waited. The whole of the hedge, with its magnificent view to the east, was now ours, but the battalion was much exhausted, and I rather feared a counter attack that night, but none came. I sent Captain Napier from the 15th Coy. to take command

LA SIGNY FARM

of the left sector, and during the night he cooperated with the 4/ N.Z.R.B. in squeezing the enemy out of the rest of the hedge on the extreme left, thus giving us command of the whole rim of the basin as far as Hébuterne. Two platoons of 2/ Wellington came up that night to be in reserve in case of emergency, and we were greatly indebted to Major Turnbull, of that battalion, for his assistance in sending up our rations that night with another party of his men.

Next morning we were able to sum up the results of the battle. Our casualties in killed and wounded were 130. We had advanced three hundred yards and exchanged a bad position for a very strong one. We counted 140 dead Huns on the sector, and had taken about 150 prisoners, with 13 heavy machine guns, 29 light machine guns, 1 Lewis gun and 2 light minenwerfers. It was a most striking success, especially in view of the fact that the men were greatly fatigued, and that the enemy were flushed with the success of their offensive. It was, I believe, the first successful attack made since that offensive had started. Cap-

LA SIGNY FARM

tains McFarland and Napier received Military Crosses for their work in the attack, Sergeant-Major Moss (16th Coy.) and Sergeant Buckthought (3rd Coy.) the D.C.M., and there was quite a shower of Military Medals. Sergeant Proctor (3rd Coy.) also received a D.C.M. in the next dispatch for his work on this occasion. To signalise the specially good work done by the battalion, I was given a bar to my D.S.O.

CHAPTER VI

THE PURPLE LINE

THE following night, Easter Sunday, the 31st March, we were relieved by the 2/ Wellington, and went into reserve, with Headquarters at Courcelles-au-Bois and the companies on a line—called the Purple Line—covering Courcelles and Bertrancourt. It was only two or three miles back, but for tired men it seemed a long way. I had not had my boots off for a week, which was hard enough with my lame leg, but I had had a dry dug-out. Some of the men had been in mud all the time, their feet were swollen, and walking was difficult, but somehow we all got back to the hot meal that was waiting for us. Stewart had snared some chickens for Headquarters, and as I ate my share at 2 o'clock in the morning I thought I had never tasted anything so good.

During our whole period in the trenches our losses had been 200. Casualties to officers were rather heavy. The 3rd Coy, had lost all

THE PURPLE LINE

its subalterns wounded—Lieuts. Farrell, Hanna, Speight and Smith. The 6th lost Lieut. Garroway wounded. The 15th, Capt. McArthur and Lieuts. Cox and Laidlaw killed. The 16th, Capts. McFarland and Johnston and Lieuts. Cox and Hogg wounded. Lieut. Nicholls now commanded the 16th for a time, and Capt. Napier the 15th.

While we had been in the front line, a great defensive system of trenches in rear had been planned and commenced, and though most of the work was done at subsequent times it will be convenient to describe it now. The front system of trenches was known as the Green Line system, and was usually occupied on our Divisional front by four battalions in the front line—two from each of the Brigades in the line. The Green Line system consisted of the Green Dotted Line, which was the outpost line of trenches held by the four front line battalions, and further back the Green Line, which was the main line of resistance of those battalions. Some three thousand yards behind the front line was the Purple Line system, a second strong defensive line, in which,

THE PURPLE LINE

or in trenches between it and the Green Line, were the other four battalions of the two Brigades in the line, one each in support and one each in reserve. Partly in the Purple Line, or sometimes altogether behind it, was the remaining Brigade of the Division, in reserve. Behind the Purple Line again, another defensive system, called the Red Line, was dug, and behind that again another line, and there may have been yet others further back beyond the ken of front area troops. Each of these lines was connected up with the others in front and in rear by innumerable switch trenches, so that if one part of any line was lost there was always a trench to form a line to a flank. Theoretically a battalion in support is in a defensive position, and fights on the spot where it is, while battalions in reserve are for counter attack. Each defensive system was guarded by masses of wire entanglements, our own Maori Pioneer battalion alone putting up many miles of wire in a wonderfully short time.

When we went to Courcelles, heaquarters were in the village, and the battalion occupied

THE PURPLE LINE

some 2000 yards of the Purple Line, which then consisted only of short lengths of trenches, which were afterwards connected up.

On the 5th April the Hun made a great attack on a wide front. It was the last effort of his offensive, and ended in a complete failure. All we knew of it at the time was from the heavy bombardment, which commenced about 5.30 a.m. This bombardment extended to a considerable depth, and seemed especially concentrated on villages and other places affording cover for troops. Courcelles got a very heavy pounding, and after breakfast I thought it discreet to visit the 15th Coy., which was outside the shelled area at the windmill near Bertrancourt, and with the Padre for company dodged cautiously through the barrage and got away from the village. Once out, the difficulty was to get back, but at lunch time hunger finally mastered prudence, and we got back to find the cook had taken refuge in the cellar, and no lunch was available. In spite of the heavy shelling we only had four casualties, one of them being the Signalling Officer, Lieut. Abel, who had only just rejoined us from a school.

THE PURPLE LINE

The same day we were reinforced with a large draft which included Lieuts. Ashton, Thomas, Walker and Caughey. We had already received a draft on the 1st April with Lieuts. Clapham, Learwood and McAdam, and so were again well up to strength. On the 7th April Capt. Wood and Lieuts. Brook, Hessall, Crawford and Hobson reported for duty, and on the 8th Major Sinel and Lieuts, Webster and Somers. Almost all the officers with these drafts had had previous service, either with the 4th Brigade, which had been formed in the summer of 1917 and was broken up in the winter, or as former N.C.O.'s of the battalion who had been sent away to New Zealand or to officer cadet units in England for training, and had received commissions. Such officers were very markedly superior to those who came direct from New Zealand with reinforcement drafts, who, of course, had no previous training in the field, and who had to learn all the practical details of warfare which no experience under other conditions can teach. The wisdom of making all promotions to commissioned rank at this stage

THE PURPLE LINE

from among those who had seen service was very apparent; in fact, it was mainly due to the excellence of the steady supply of promoted N.C.O.'s, who rejoined during the summer and autumn on completion of their schools, that the high standard of the Division was maintained throughout the autumn in spite of our heavy casualties.

Of the officers who had just joined us, Lieut. Hessall went to the 16th Coy., which he now commanded for a short time, and Capt. Wood went to work with Stewart at the Q.M. stores; shortly after Capt. Wood became Quartermaster and Stewart went to command the 16th Coy. with Hessall as his second in command. Major Sinel became second in command of the battalion and Major Shepherd went to the Rifle Brigade. The latter was a distinct loss to us. Though only a short time with the battalion, it had been a very critical period and his advice and help had been of much value. Major Sinel had originally left New Zealand with the Main Body and was wounded on Gallipoli. He had returned to New Zealand and came back again as second in command

THE PURPLE LINE

of the 3rd Battalion, in the days of the 4th Brigade. He was a man of very great personal courage and considerable energy.

Since we had arrived in this part of the country the Quartermaster's store and transport with our two bands, had been living at Acheux in billets, but were now moved to a place near the windmill at Louvencourt where they remained for several weeks. From this period it was the custom each time when the battalion was in the front trenches, for either the Company Commander or second in command of each Company to go to live at the Transport Lines, while the others went into the trenches with not more than three platoon officers from each company. The same applied to the Battalion Commander and second in command, in theory, but in practice I always avoided staying out and the only times when Major Sinel went into the trenches with the battalion were when I was on leave or wounded. In addition to the officers left at the Transport Lines, a number of N.C.O.'s were left out, and a proportion of signallers, Lewis gunners and others possessing special

THE PURPLE LINE

technical knowledge; the object being to have a nucleus of trained men in every department on which to build up the battalion again in case of heavy casualties.

CHAPTER VII

TRENCH WARFARE

THE battlion stayed in the Purple Line till the afternoon of April 9th, when in very wet weather we relieved the 2/ N.Z.R.B., commanded by Colonel Jardine, and went into the front line. The battalion front was the hedge at La Signy Farm from " Waterloo Bridge " to a point nearly half-way to Hébuterne, a long front on which it was necessary to use three Companies—the 3rd, 15th and 6th, in that order—with the 16th in reserve. Colonel Jardine had made his Headquarters in a miserable hole in the ground half-way back to Colincamps. I spent one wretched night there, and then moved to a dug-out just beside our old Headquarters near the Sugar Factory, which was now occupied by 1/ Wellington. Headquarters was now behind the extreme right of the battalion front, but it was at a point which was easily found by runners on a dark night, and the right of the sector was really the key of our position.

TRENCH WARFARE

This period was quite uneventful except that on the 11th Capt. Napier's dug-out was unluckily hit by a 5.9 shell, which shook him badly and killed his Company Sergt.-Major Brown, a very valuable man. Capt. Napier had to be evacuated, but rejoined on the 17th, and meanwhile the 15th Coy. was commanded by Lieut. (later temp.-Capt.) Harrison.

2/ Wellington relieved us on the 14th, and we moved back to the support line, with Headquarters by the road from Colincamps a few hundred yards out of that village, and the battalion in a line of platoon posts from behind the Sugar Factory on the Serre Road to near Sailly. This support line formed a defensive position intermediate between the Green and Purple Lines. It was a good home in which we spent four very peaceful days. On the afternoon of the 16th the Hun put a shell into Euston dump, which exploded a pile of Stokes mortars and "plum pudding" bombs, blowing an enormous crater.

2/ Canterbury relieved us on the 17th, and we moved back to a camp south of Bertrancourt. Here tarpaulin shelters had been

TRENCH WARFARE

erected, and every one was under cover, but we were near some 6-inch and 8-inch howitzer batteries, which had a disturbing habit of firing short bursts during the night whenever we were falling asleep. The weather turned wet and cold, and our rest was not a great pleasure, but we had time to get everyone bathed and into clean clothing again. While here the Brigade was in reserve. On the 22nd April, Major Sherson joined us and commanded the 3rd Coy. *vice* Capt. Paterson, who was returning to New Zealand.

Our next move was to a new sector. I have mentioned a Brigade of the 4th Australian Division that had come in on our left and was sandwiched in between us and the 42nd Division. This Brigade was to go out and rejoin its own Division somewhere in the south, our Brigade replacing it, while the right Brigade of our Division was to be relieved by some troops further south—our whole Division thus side-slipping one Brigade front northwards. 2/Wellington were to go into the front line of the right of this sector, and 1/ Auckland on the left in front of Hébuterne, so that the right

TRENCH WARFARE

of 2/ Wellington was now to be where our left had been when we were last in the line. We were to go into support, holding a line in rear of the left of 2/ Wellington and running through the middle of Hébuterne behind 1/ Auckland, The relief involved one Brigade of the 42nd Division moving out of Hébuterne, as our Brigade was very strong and able to hold considerably more ground than the Australians had done. My own share of the relief was somewhat complicated, as I had to take over from two and a-half battalions of English troops and one of Australians, which practically amounted to each company relieving one battalion. To effect the relief we moved to Sailly-au-Bois on the 23rd April, and took over from the 13th Australian Battalion, becoming the reserve battalion to the Australian Brigade. The following day we moved to Hébuterne and completed all our relief, and had settled down early in the afternoon. Headquarters was in a cellar close to the catacombs with the Orderly Room in the catacombs themselves. In all the villages in this part of France so-called catacombs exist, which

TRENCH WARFARE

are really quarries out of which has been mined many years ago the chalk with which most of the buildings are made. In most places the entrances to these quarries have been lost, and the memory of the oldest inhabitant did not go back far enough to trace them. Many of them were found by our Engineers, and perhaps the best specimen was at Sailly-au Bois, where galleries on two levels penetrated to considerable distances and made a fairly comfortable home. The catacombs at Hébuterne were a particularly vile specimen of their class. They had been discovered by British troops in earlier days, and had probably sufficient accommodation for a battalion. They were entered by climbing down a steep flight of about seventy steps, and had several shafts for ventilation, but they were wet and dismal, and we used them as little as possible. It seemed better to be killed by a shell on top than to die slowly of trench fever or other diseases bred by the gloom below, and besides I could only climb up and down the stairs with difficulty. Here we had all the four companies in one line, headquarters just in rear, and the

TRENCH WARFARE

R.A.P. in another cellar on the road to Fonquevillers. Brigade and the reserve battalion were at Sailly. We were not uncomfortable in this position, and had no casualties.

On the 30th April we relieved 2/ Wellington in the right half of the Brigade sector, putting the 6th Coy. on the right and the 16th on the left, with the 3rd and 15th in support and reserve. Our position in this sector was an extremely strong one—the front line running along the rim of the basin from Hébuterne towards La Signy Farm, and giving us splendid observation over the basin towards Puisieux and Rossignol Wood. In fact it was impossible for any Hun within a mile to move without being seen, while behind us none of the ground was exposed to his view. Headquarters was in a deep dug-out near the road from Sailly to Hébuterne. This dug-out was another relic of 1916, but 2/ Wellington had started improvements to it, which we carried on, which made it a fairly good place to live in. By this time Lieut.-Col. Cunningham had come out from England, where he had been on a tour of duty at Sling, and had

TRENCH WARFARE

taken over the 2/ Wellington battalion from Major Turnbull, who became 2nd in command. In the 1st Brigade it was the custom for 2/ Auckland and 2/ Wellington to relieve one another, and it was always a great pleasure to work with Lieut.-Col. Cunningham. He was a far-seeing man of cool judgment and an excellent type to work with, so that our mutual reliefs were always easily effected, and in any work on our sector we had a continuity of policy between the two battalions which did not always exist elsewhere. This period in the front line was quite uneventful, except for a little affair in the sunken road which marked our left flank, through which Corporal Baker got a Military Medal.

On the 2nd May, a reinforcement draft joined us which included 2/ Lieuts. W. J. R. Hill, Raymond, McCreanor, Vickerman and Lane. Raymond became Transport Officer in place of Ruddock, who returned to England for a tour of duty shortly after.

The 1st Brigade went into reserve again on the 6th May, 2/ Canterbury taking our place while we moved to the Purple Line with head-

TRENCH WARFARE

quarters at the Windmill near Bertrancourt, and the battalion stretched over a very long line from near Beaussart in front of Courcelles to a point nearly half-way from Courcelles to Sailly. While here Lieuts. Porritt and Kingsford both " went sick," and afterwards were sent to England, where they remained on duty at Sling. A few days later Lieut. Brook also went. The weather had greatly improved by now, and before the end of the month became oppressively hot.

On the 12th May the 1st Brigade relieved the Rifle Brigade on the right subsector of the Divisional front. We relieved the 2/ N.Z.R.B. in reserve. The battalion was distributed with two companies, one on either side of Colincamps and two further to the left. Headquarters was in some " elephant iron " dugouts placed in the side of a cutting, and was the best we ever had in this neighbourhood, as there were no steps to descend and we were warm and dry. The whole battalion was very comfortable. An enemy attack on our front was daily expected during this period, but no one seemed much perturbed at the prospect,

TRENCH WARFARE

as by now we had made the whole section as strong as it could possibly be with trenches and barbed wire.

On the 18th May we again relieved 2/Wellington, going back into our old front line position at La Signy Farm, with the 3rd and 15th Companies in the front line, the 6th in support, and the 16th in reserve. We completed two fine pieces of digging; one of them, started by 2/Wellington, a reserve line where the 16th Coy. lived, and the other, a new front line trench connecting Central Avenue and Northern Avenue on the 15th Coy. front, and cutting off a re-entrant in our line. I had a scheme of digging in view which I believe would have turned the Huns out of La Signy Farm, but it was never finished, as we did not return to this sector again. While here we had our only experience in the battalion of being raided by the enemy, and his attempt was a complete failure. It occurred one morning just before daylight. I was lying comfortably tucked into my bunk when I heard the guns firing, and half guessing what was happening, wondered whether the occa-

TRENCH WARFARE

sion demanded that I should put on my boots and go out. The telephone rang, and I heard the Artillery liaison officer answering some questions over it. He said, " These people don't seem to be taking much notice of it," but perhaps he did not make allowance for the natural reluctance to turn out in the early morning. However, I decided decency demanded an interest should be taken in what was occurring, and presently Captain Tuck (aroused with difficulty) and I sallied out as the day dawned and the shooting faded away. On reaching the front we found that the Hun had tried to raid our salient in Central Avenue. I had considered this a weak place, and had been wiring in the gap between Railway and Central Avenues on the right while digging on the left to connect Central and Northern Avenues. The raiders had been surprised by running into the covering party, protecting the wiring party, who opened fire with a Lewis gun. We found afterwards two dead Huns, from whom we got identifications, and six German rifles, no doubt dropped by others of the party. Our casualties were only two or three

TRENCH WARFARE

from shell fire, and of course we lost no one prisoner, so that the raid had failed entirely.

Owing to a bombardment of Fonquevillers a few days previously with mustard gas shell, the Division on our left had sustained considerable loss, and it was considered that training in the wearing of box respirators for a long period had not been carried out to a sufficient extent. We were therefore ordered to wear box respirators for an hour a day on several successive days, a practice which was useful but unpleasant. Wearing a box respirator for a short time is easy, but after the first half-hour the constriction of the scalp by the elastic which passes round the head to hold on the mask causes much discomfort. One of these practice periods fell on the evening of 24th May, when we were relieved by 2/ Canterbury, and I had hoped to get to our billets before the time arrived for it, but owing to that battalion arriving late we were caught on the march and had to finish it with the box respirators on. No doubt this was valuable training, but that it should happen on the march was unnecessary and annoying, especially as

TRENCH WARFARE

that battalion had already on several occasions when relieving us shown no consideration for our convenience. This, however, was quite different later on, when Lieut.-Col. H. Stewart resumed command of 2/ Canterbury, from which he had been incapacitated for a time by hay fever.

When relieved on this occasion we moved out to billets at St. Leger Authie, and although the billets were far from good, the accommodation was far superior to anything we had had for a long time. We remained at St. Leger until the 1st June, spending our eight days' rest very pleasantly, although we were busy training through the whole period. During a long period in the trenches, the smartness of a battalion gets lost, and it takes a day or two to get back to that state of polish and efficiency which should characterise a good battalion. The men enjoyed their holiday from trench warfare and went to work at their training with a will. According to the report of the Brigade Major a certain excessive exuberance was developed in some of the bolder spirits, which resulted in what Colonel Cunningham

TRENCH WARFARE

used to call the "Battle of Authie," an affair which was harmless enough but for which 1st and 2/ Auckland and 2/ Wellington received undeserved censure from higher authority. I firmly believe that the real, as distinguished from the imaginary portion of this "battle" was caused entirely by men from the Entrenching Group, who celebrated in Authie the night following a pay day.

While at St. Leger, every man in the battalion went through a course of musketry, and we ended with a "battalion in attack" field day in which we were much criticised by the Brigadier, though in the light of subsequent events in real warfare I should do exactly the same again, and am sure I was quite right. The disadvantage of mimic warfare is always that the person carrying out a manœuvre gets from his orders a different idea of the operation from what the one who ordered it intended. Imaginary events are introduced while the attack is in progress which cause a further conflict of ideas, which would not occur to such an extent in a real operation with hostile troops to furnish a

TRENCH WARFARE

criterion with which to test the different interpretation given to the various incidents.

The most notable occurence of our stay at St. Leger, was the Brigade Transport competition and horse show which was held near Vauchelles. The whole Brigade marched over to it, and on such a beautiful summer day it was a most enjoyable function. The 2/ Auckland transport was most successful on this occasion, winning first prizes for the best complete transport and for almost every vehicle turned out. It was an extraordinary and most gratifying success for us, and following also on the Transport show of 1917 at Strazeele in which we had shared the honours fairly evenly with 1/ Auckland. The Cup which we won for the battalion transport was presented by General Melvill, and it is hoped that some day it will be competed for by the territorial battalions in the Auckland district. The greatest credit for our success was due to Major Sinel and the battalion Transport Officer, Lieut. Raymond, who had spared no pains to work everything up to the best standard.

TRENCH WARFARE

On the 1st June we left St. Leger with great regret and marched to Sailly, where we relieved the 3/ N.Z.R.B.—the Brigade taking over the left (Hébuterne) sector of the Divisional front, with ourselves as battalion in reserve. This was a most comfortable position, with headquarters in the cellars of a house in the village and the battalion in dugouts and trenches in rear of the village extending from near the road to Couin towards the Château de la Haie, one company being in cellars in the village. Only one incident worth recording marked our stay here; this was the shelling of the village with gas shells for half an hour one night. About one o'clock I woke up and noticed the gas and got everyone roused and into their gas masks before the gas sentry, who must have been asleep I think, had appeared to warn us. The shells were mostly of the comparatively harmless "Blue Cross" lachrymatory variety, with some of the "Green Cross" phosgene shells among them. It was rather interesting, and its only result was to disturb our sleep. Capt. Tuck and I walked along to Brigade head-

TRENCH WARFARE

quarters in the catacombs in Sailly and by the time we got back the shelling was over.

CHAPTER VIII

AT REST AND MORE TRENCH WARFARE

IT was now decided to take out the whole Division into reserve for a rest, and on the 6th June we were relieved by a battalion of the 52nd Division, the 8th Lancashire Fusiliers and moved to our old home in the Purple Line with headquarters at the windmill between Bertrancourt and Courcelles. The battalion remained here for a few days, then moved to Couin, and finally to a very comfortable hutted camp at Vauchelles. Meanwhile I took a step I had had in view for some time and went to England where I got married. On this occasion the battalion gave me a most beautiful wedding present which I value very highly. I have always appreciated the honour of commanding such men as have been in the 2/ Auckland Regt. and the gift of this present made me feel that I had gained something of their confidence and esteem in return.

AT REST AND MORE TRENCH WARFARE

On the 8th June General Russell very kindly sent me to Boulogne in a car from Division, and I crossed to England next day. Being much delayed by vicissitudes of travel on the return journey, I only succeeded in rejoining the battalion on the 27th June when they were at Vauchelles. Major Sinel had commanded the battalion meanwhile, and the usual course of training had been carried out. Unfortunately a severe epidemic of influenza had broken out in the Division, and we had many cases, a large part of our camp being turned into a hospital for them. These cases did not take a serious turn, and were admirably cared for by Dr. Harpur and Major Sinel. When we finally left Vauchelles a hospital camp was started in Marieux Wood to which the influenza cases were sent.

When the Division went back into the line again, it side-slipped one whole Brigade front northwards, so that its frontage extended from a point North of La Signy farm to Biez Wood. This frontage gave us the Gommecourt sector for the left Brigade in the line. This was a most interesting sector. Gommecourt had

AT REST AND MORE TRENCH WARFARE

marked the most Western point of the old German front line from 1914 to 1917. The salient formed by the village and wood had projected between the two British salients at Hébuterne and Fonquevilles and formed naturally a very strong position which the German engineers had rendered still more formidable by art. In 1916 at the opening of the Somme battle it was attempted to capture Gommecourt, but the attack had ended in failure. The enemy had abandoned the place when they retreated in 1917 and their advance in March, 1918, had not quite reached it, and it remained a mile inside our line. The old trenches and dugouts were now in many cases intact, as was also a long tunnel driven under the village and wood, which had led from the former battalion or regimental commander's dug-out behind the wood for some seven or eight hundred yards through to the support trenches in front. No doubt this tunnel had largely contributed to the failure of our attack in 1916.

The front trenches of our new Brigade sector ran from the left of our old front at Hébut-

AT REST AND MORE TRENCH WARFARE

erne to a point close to the Western edge of Rossignol Wood, which the Huns now held, then turned East and ran along Railway Trench parallel to the North side of the wood, then North again and skirted the Eastern corner of Biez Wood.

This was the sector which the 1st Brigade was to take over, 2/Auckland relieving the 1/5 Loyal North Lancashire Regt. on the left of the sector from Railway Trench, inclusive, to Biez Wood.

We reconnoitred the trenches on Sunday, 30th June, the company commanders and myself, with one or two others going by motor lorries to Souastre and walking thence through Fonquevillers and Gommecourt to the battalion headquarters in Salmon Trench. Unfortunately we missed the celebrated Church Parade at which Mr. Massey and Sir Joseph Ward were present, which gave rise to several ludicrous incidents which those who were there will remember. The battalion moved into the trenches next day, going by motor lorry to Souastre, marching to a point near Fonquevillers, where we halted for tea, carry-

AT REST AND MORE TRENCH WARFARE

ing out the relief in the evening. The battalion transport moved meanwhile to the valley between St. Leger Authie and Couin. Our new position was not nearly so good as our old ones had been. Railway Trench was isolated, not being connected with our other trenches on its flanks so that a gap of 100 yards existed in our front line between it and Ash Trench which ran parallel to it. From Ash Trench our front was continuous along Bass Trench to Biez Wood. The 15th and 16th Coys. went into the front line under Harrison and Stewart, the 15th holding Railway and Ash Trenches and the 16th Bass Trench. The 6th Coy. under Captain Moncrief were in support in Chub Trench, Headquarters behind them again in Salmon Trench, and the 3rd Coy. under Major Sherson in reserve in Tram Trench. The trenches were in bad order for the most part and needed much work done on them. I set a party to work by night to dig a new trench to connect Railway and Ash Trenches, a work which we finished before we left, in a very thorough manner. Nothing of much interest occurred during this

AT REST AND MORE TRENCH WARFARE

period. Lieut. Ryder was wounded but otherwise our losses were very slight. The influenza epidemic died out, and we began to get a number of men back from Marieux Wood Hospital Camp.

On the 9th July the Brigade went into Divisional reserve. We were relieved by 2/ Canterbury and moved to the hutted camp at Coigneux. This was a very comfortable place to live in, the whole battalion was well concentrated and we were within easy distance of the rest of the Brigade and of our own Transport lines and Quartermaster's store About this time Capt. Wood went to the 3rd Coy. as second in command to Major Sherson, in succession to Capt. Derrom, who had gone to England, and Lieut. Hessall became Quartermaster. Major McClelland rejoined the battalion after a long absence in England and took command of the 16th Coy. with Capt. Stewart as his second in command, and Lieut. King joined us from the Machine Gun battalion as Signalling officer. Lieut. Hewitt also rejoined after two years away from us. The weather was very hot and oppresive with the

AT REST AND MORE TRENCH WARFARE

frequent thunderstorms that characterise the summer of France.

While we were at Coigneux, a fine stroke was made against the enemy by the N.Z.R.B. in front of Hébuterne, in which they took Fusilier trench, which ran over a high shoulder of ground forming a salient into our line between Hébuterne and Rossignol Wood. This operation paved the way for several small advances made in the next fortnight.

Our Brigade relieved the Rifle Brigade at Hébuterne on the 17th, 2/ Auckland going into Brigade reserve at Sailly. The battalion was in the same position as when last in reserve at Sailly except that Headquarters was now in a house on the Coigneux-Sailly road which had been a former Brigade headquarters. Before moving from here we were joined by a Company of the 317th U.S.A. Regiment which was attached to us for training. I re-formed each of my companies into three platoons and attached to each Company a platoon of the Americans. They joined us on the 25th July and the same evening we relieved 2/ Wellington as the right bat-

AT REST AND MORE TRENCH WARFARE

talion of the Brigade in the trenches immediately in front of Hébuterne. While in these trenches, 2/ Wellington had improved on the success of the Rifle Brigade and pushed forward to Chasseur Hedge, and the 2nd Brigade on their left had turned the Huns out of Rossignol Wood. 1/ Auckland also had advanced along the old German 1916 front line—Nameless Trench and Nameless Support—for some distance. 2/ Wellington took over the extreme end of these trenches with one platoon, which was rather isolated, as there was no trench across the 300 yards of old "No Man's Land" which separated them from the rest of their front in Chasseur Hedge. We relieved 2/ Wellington while the Huns were making a counter attack against 1/ Auckland on the left which resulted in a complete failure, many Huns being made prisoner.

There was a great deal of rain during our eight days in this position, which certainly gave the Americans experience in working in muddy trenches. They were a very fine lot of fellows whom it was quite a pleasure to have with us. They were always ready for

AT REST AND MORE TRENCH WARFARE

their full share of the work, and more, and most anxious to learn all they could in the short time they were with us. Sometimes they were most amusing. While doing my usual morning round of the trenches the first day in, I stopped to talk to one of their officers, who, when I was going, asked me to "just snap around any time," as he would always be pleased to see me. On the other hand I found it had a most shattering effect on my nerves to pass one particular corner every morning where an American invariably had me covered with his rifle. It seemed impossible to teach him in which direction the enemy were, and I doubt if he really understood English. Perhaps the most remarkable point about the Americans was the ease with which they got lost. They could never find the way anywhere, which was the more extraordinary because these with us were country bred from Virginia, but perhaps the high percentage of illiteracy among the Virginians accounts for it to some extent. On the 29th this Company left us, but were followed the same day by a second Company

AT REST AND MORE TRENCH WARFARE

from the same Regiment who stayed till the 2nd August. Capt. Peterson, who commanded this second company, appeared a particularly fine type of officer of marked capacity.

Except for the American visit, this period in the trenches was uneventful. It was decided not to push forward any further, and even to abandon Chasseur Hedge and make Jena Trench our front line. This was accordingly done, the dugouts in the Hedge being blown up by the Engineers when we retired. To connect up our isolated platoon in Nameless Trench, we dug a very fine new trench across from Jena, a very solid piece of work. Lieut. Caughey was wounded, and Lieut. Hobson left for New Zealand. We had the 3rd and 6th Companys in the front line, with the 16th in support and 15th in reserve.

1/ Canterbury relieved us and the Brigade went into reserve again on the 2nd August, 2/ Auckland moving to the Château de la Haie switch trench with Headquarters in the catacombs at Sailly and companies on a line

AT REST AND MORE TRENCH WARFARE

running round the Eastern edge of Sailly and towards the Château de la Haie on the left. Here we spent a very pleasant and uneventful eight days. We were joined on the 5th by Lieuts. Worsley, Peace, Lang, Garroway, and Cooper. On the 10th it was the turn of the 1st Brigade to relieve the N.Z.R.B. on the left Brigade sector at Gommecourt, 2/ Auckland going into the support line and relieving the 3/ N.Z.R.B. We were just going to move from Sailly after lunch, when a shell burst over our headquarters mess, and Capt. Tuck failed to avoid a small splinter which caught him in the shoulder and inflicted a very slight wound. However slight a wound may be it is necessary for the injured man to have an injection of A.T.S. (Anti-Tetanus Serum) and Capt. Tuck went back to the Field Ambulance for this, rejoining us later in the day at Gommecourt. The long walk following the A.T.S. caused the effect of the injection to be very severe, and he was ill for several days during which his temper made it unsafe to go near him, and I afterwards sent him on leave so that he missed the exciting events

AT REST AND MORE TRENCH WARFARE

which followed in a fortnight's time. Meanwhile Lieut. Nicholls, assistant adjutant, carried on as adjutant in Capt. Tuck's place.

The Support Trenches at Gommecourt ran East of the wood and village, with Headquarters in the old German command dugout, from underneath which ran the subterranean gallery I have mentioned before. We were joined on the 12th August by Lieuts. Hill, Taylor, Carnahan, and Popple.

We were due to relieve 2/ Wellington on the right battalion front, that is the Rossignol Wood sector on the 18th, and on the morning of the 17th I went with Capt. Tuck to Colonel Cunningham's headquarters at Salmon Point to arrange the details of the relief. He told me that early in the morning the Huns had retired from their front trenches opposite 2/ Wellington, and also from the front of the 2nd Brigade on their right. Patrols had pushed forward for some distance and at that moment he was busy writing orders for an advance of two of his companies to gain touch with the enemy and follow up the retirement. To see what eventuated, Capt. Tuck and I went

AT REST AND MORE TRENCH WARFARE

on to the front, and past our front of yesterday to La Louviere farm and on along the road towards Puisieux. Selecting a point of vantage we watched 2/ Wellington advance towards Puisieux, and further to the right, parties from the 2nd Brigade move forward up the rising ground towards Serre. The enemy opened a desultory fire with two or three guns on our advance, without doing much harm. Machine gun fire from Puisieux however, checked the Wellington advance before they reached the ruins of that town, and incidentally made our view point unpleasant, so we returned to our own battalion. The result of the advance that day and the following night and day was that our line on our extreme left remained stationary, and pivoted on a point near Bucquoy while our right swung round to the East of Serre, the 2nd Brigade holding the front from Serre to Puisieux and the first Brigade from Puisieux to Bucquoy. A minor operation near Bucquoy in conjunction with the 37th Division on our left materially improved our position.

AT REST AND MORE TRENCH WARFARE

The Brigade front had somewhat contracted as a result of these operations, and in the relief on the 18th it was decided to hold the Brigade front with one battalion only—1/ Wellington—while 2/ Auckland relieved the rear companies of 1/ Auckland and 2/ Wellington and held a second line. This was a prelude to an operation on a large scale which had been prepared very secretly on this part of the front with the primary object of seizing Bapaume.

CHAPTER IX

GREVILLERS

THE relief of the 18th August marked the close of trench warfare to which we had been accustomed for so long. A very different phase was now to begin, and to continue for the rest of the war as far as we were concerned, except for a short relapse into conditions of trench warfare south of Havrincourt Wood in September. The period of open warfare was now to be ushered in, a time to which many had looked forward for long, but which had seemed a hopeless prospect to others who thought that the stalemate of trench warfare would endure to the end. We did not dream at the time, however, on the eve of what great events we were standing.

The first we heard of the great attack that was planned for the 21st August, was when the Padre returned from Boulogne a week before, and brought back a circumstantial account from the base that was hardly believed. A few days later our own artillery confirmed

GREVILLERS

the rumour, but we only heard definitely from our Brigade on the 19th, when the attack was about to be delivered. All preparations were made with the greatest secrecy. Movements of troops were made entirely by night and no preparations that could possibly attract the enemy's attention were made. The final arrangements were completed on the night of the 20th August, guns moved up to their positions for the barrage, and the troops for the attack assembled. The task of the New Zealand Division in the first phase was a very small one. Only the Rifle Brigade which was now holding the trenches on our right was to take part, and that only in a minor degree. On our front the attacking troops were the 5th Division, which had now just marched down from the North. To make room for them that night, we squeezed ourselves into a very small area close to Salmon Point, and gave up all the rest, into which the Brigade of the 5th Division moved in the evening. The Pioneer Battalion of the Division planted itself round my battalion headquarters and made all movements for the next day or two very

GREVILLERS

difficult. It was extremely annoying to have them there, as it was outside their area, but there seemed no place for them to go to, so we had to endure it !

The attack commenced on the 21st August just as it began to grow a little light. There was no preliminary bombardment so as to effect a complete surprise, but a great mass of artillery was collected for the barrage and for shooting into the back areas. A long row of 4.5 howitzers fired from just behind Salmon Point, but moved forward later in the day. The morning was remarkable for a very thick fog, which hardly cleared off all day, and remained quite thick all morning. This fog no doubt protected the advance of our troops, but was also responsible for hindering communication and for much loss of touch and direction by the attacking troops. The objectives given had not been so limited as used to be the case in our earlier attacks, and for a considerable time there was much uncertainty as to the line reached, though it was soon known that the attack was highly successful. In the afternoon all battalions in the Brigade were con-

GREVILLERS

centrated between Gommecourt and Salmon Point, and we expected to move every moment. That night, however, and the next we remained undisturbed.

On the morning of the 22nd the Commanding Officers and Company Commanders of the 1st Brigade were ordered to meet General Russell and the Brigadier at Ablainzeville, a mile or two to the North. There we were ordered to reconnoitre the position captured by the 63rd Division at Logeast Wood in view of the probability of our being ordered in at this point to take Achiet-le-Grand and Bihucourt. This was not to be the case, however, and as a matter of fact these places were taken the following night by the 37th Division, I believe.

On the 23rd August, about half past three in the afternoon, Brigade telephoned us to be on the road between Rossignol Wood and Bucquoy in an hour, and that the Brigade was moving in the direction of Achiet-le-Petit, with 2/ Auckland leading. It was an inconvenient time as the men were in the middle of their tea, but we got on to the road where we received our orders to move through Bucquoy

GREVILLERS

to a point on the road from that place to Achiet-le-Petit where the Brigade would concentrate. We moved forward without any mishap and reached the point indicated where we found good cover from shell fire in some old German trenches on the left of the road, with one or two small shelters on the right, where we put battalion headquarters. Unfortunately before we had got well under cover, two or three large shells came over, and one of them caused several casualties among the 3rd Coy. Signallers. We were joined here by our transport which camped in the hollow behind us, and we set to work to make the best of our new home.

About ten o'clock I was roused by a guide to take myself and Lieut. Nicholls (who was acting as adjutant) to a conference to be held at 2/Wellington headquarters. It was a dark night and the place was hard to find, but eventually all the Commanding Officers were collected, and General Melvill gave us our orders and explained the situation. At this time our line, held by the 5th Division ran a little east of the Albert-Arras railway about midway be-

GREVILLERS

tween Achiet-le-Petit and Grevillers. On the left the 37th Division held Bihucourt. The next objective was a line including Loupart Wood, Grevillers and Biefvillers, but even at this late hour it was uncertain what our exact task was to be. There were two alternative schemes. The first was for our Brigade to seize the line Loupart Wood-Grevillers, after which the 2nd Brigade would pass through and commence the encirclement of Bapaume; the second was, that in case a Brigade of the 5th Division took Loupart Wood and Grevillers we were to pass through them. In the latter case 2/ Auckland were to pass round the North of Bapaume, forming an advance guard for the Brigade; and in the former and more probable case 2/ Auckland were to take the objective from Grevillers inclusive to the railway on the edge of Biefvillers, while 1/ Wellington on the right took Loupart Wood, with 2/ Wellington in support and 1/ Auckland remaining in reserve—and this is what ultimately took place. Some description of the ground will now make the narrative clearer.

GREVILLERS

The ground is fairy elevated, open country, the only enclosures or trees being around the different villages, each of which is hidden away in the grove that surrounds it. There is a succession of low ridges, like waves, from Bucquoy eastward through Bapaume—and to a considerable distance beyond, the ridges running north and south. In one of the corresponding hollows east of Achiet-le-Petit runs the railway from Albert up the Ancre Valley through Achiet-le-Grand to Arras. Our outposts were now on top of the crest east of this railway. East of this crest again was a wide, shallow depression, in which were the enemy outposts, and on the far side of this again another low rise running through Loupart Wood, Grevillers and Biefvillers, though most of Grevillers lay on the reverse side of the ridge, and ran back into the hollow beyond. A road running direct from Achiet-le-Petit to Grevillers marked the boundary for the advance between 1/ Wellington and 2/ Auckland. From the railway junction at Achiet-le-Grand a line runs east between Grevillers and Biefvillers to Bapaume, and

GREVILLERS

marked the left of 2/ Auckland. The road from Achiet-le-Petit to Grevillers crosses the Albert-Arras railway, and ascends the rise on the other side, on top of which were the 5th Division outposts. On top of the ridge it is joined at a point which I called the "Starfish" by roads from Achiet-le-Grand and Bihucourt on the left, and from Irles on the right, and the Bihucourt Road marked roughly the line of our outposts, and was the line on which we prepared to form for the attack, with our right on the road to Grevillers and our left on the railway to Bapaume.

I got back to the battalion after the conference just before midnight, collected the company commanders and the officer commanding the section of Vickers guns which was attached to the battalion for the attack, and explained the situation to them. This was difficult, as a candle would not burn steadily enough in the open to see the map by its light, but finally we managed to crowd together in a very tiny dugout. The scheme for the attack was as follows:—The 15th Company on the right was to take half the

GREVILLERS

frontage of the attack and advance on Grevillers; as they reached Grevillers they were to open out and two platoons move round through the outskirts of the village to the right and two to the left, all working round Grevillers, till finally gaining touch with one another again on the farther side of the village, they were to reach the final objective just beyond. The 3rd Company was to follow the 15th, and, as the 15th opened out, to fill up the gap and take the village of Grevillers, the 16th Company to take the left half of the frontage—between Biefvillers and Grevillers—and move straight on to the final objective. The 6th Company to be in reserve and move with battalion headquarters to a position in rear of the crest between Biefvillers and Grevillers. Headquarters was to move forward as the attack progressed and be established at a point close to the road from Bihucourt to Grevillers, where that road was crossed by a track from Biefvillers; it would then be at an unmistakable point which could easily be found by runners. The Vickers guns were to cover our left flank.

GREVILLERS

It should be mentioned that the officers commanding the companies on this occasion were Capt. Wood, Capt. Moncrief, Lieut. Clapham, and Major McClelland. The doctor, Capt. Harpur, was away on leave, and Capt. Simcox was taking his place temporarily.

The time for the attack had been fixed for 4.15 in the morning, and to reach our position it was necessary to move at 2 o'clock. The Battalion was on the road, ready to move, when a message came from Brigade—" 13th Brigade, 5th Division, have four battalions advancing on Loupart Wood and Grevillers. You will assemble at 4.15 a.m., as ordered. No barrage will be placed on our front, owing to 13th Brigade troops being forward. You will take final objective, as ordered. If only little resistance met with, exploit success north and east and south-west of Bapaume. Acknowledge by bearer." This message meant that after all we were to carry out the second alternative scheme mentioned above. To anticipate the actual sequence of events, however, on reaching our assembly position

GREVILLERS

we found from the 5th Division posts that none of their troops were moving forward, so in the end we carried out the first alternative after all, with this important difference, that our attack was delivered now without a barrage or any artillery support at all.

The battalion moved off in column of route, preceded by one section of the 16th Company, along the road towards Achiet-le-Petit. To avoid passing through the village, which appeared a dangerous place for shell fire, we moved to the left round its fringe, and reached the road to Grevillers on the farther side, then we kept to the road and went on across the railway (where Brigade Headquarters was to be established) to the "Starfish" cross roads. At the "Starfish" we wheeled to the left along the road to Bihucourt, and the 15th and 16th Companies took up their position on this road with Battalion Headquarters behind them; the 3rd Company formed behind the road in rear of the 15th, and the 6th Company in rear again and behind headquarters. The night was dark, but it was just possible to distinguish the trees of Loupart Wood, Gre-

GREVILLERS

villers and Biefvillers against the sky-line, so that there were good points on which to direct the flanks of the battalion attack as well as the inner flanks of the two leading Companies. Everything was curiously still. We had seen the 5th Division advanced posts near the "Starfish," but there were no posts to be found on our left, which I assumed was in advance of them, and the only sign of the presence of our troops on that flank was an occasional enemy shell bursting in Bihucourt.

We were in position about half-past three. 1/ Wellington should have been in position on our right, but there was no one there. I knew that when we attacked our left flank would be exposed, as no simultaneous attack was expected to be made by the 37th Division, but I was hardly prepared for there being no one on the right also. Moreover, the tanks which were expected to help us had not yet materialised. Considering the wide frontage on which we were attacking, I thought it inadvisable to detach any party for flank defence and so weaken the momentum of the advance; and I decided to adhere to

GREVILLERS

my plan and use every man for pushing forward, and to trust to troops moving up behind us to cover the flanks, if necessary. My work was to get forward and make good as much ground as possible.

. The general idea of the formation for the attack was for the 15th and 16th Companies to move forward with each company covering its own front with patrols, and following them up with larger and more closely formed bodies; the 3rd Company was to follow the 15th and keep in touch with them, and the 6th Company and headquarters would keep in touch with the 3rd. No party was to get out of sight of the party in front, which meant on that night keeping within an extreme distance of 150 yards, so that the whole Battalion would move forward very much concentrated.

The nearest Huns seemed to be at a point about 300 yards distant on our left front, where an enemy post was very actively firing flares towards us. From this post I expected a good deal of trouble.

1/ Wellington arrived, but were too late to attack at 4.15. We moved off punctually to the minute, but met a slight check two or three hundred yards forward from a barb-wire entanglement through or over which we had to scramble. At this moment the enemy post on our left front observed us and opened fire with several machine-guns, which enfiladed our advance, and stopped the progress of Vickerman's platoon on the extreme left of the 16th Company. The rest of the line continued to advance, and surprised two or three Hun posts on our right, taking them prisoners before they fired a shot; and, with the 6th Company and headquarters, I worked over to the right to get away from the machine-gun fire, afterwards working back gradually to the left again, and leaving the enemy post in rear. I then detached a sergeant (I think Sergt. O'Brien, of the 3rd Company) and a few men to take the machine-gun post from the rear. This was immediately successful, and the only casualties we had sustained from their fire were Lieut. Webster, a very fine officer, killed, and a lance-corporal wounded. By this time I had caught up with Major McClelland, who was actively reorganising his com-

GREVILLERS

pany in view of Vickerman's platoon being left behind, and being now too weak on the left flank I sent a platoon of the 6th Company out towards the railway. To anticipate events again, after the machine-guns were accounted for, Vickerman got his platoon forward with great boldness and gained his objective on the extreme left. After this machine-gun nest had been cleared up we met with no opposition for some time. The Huns were completely surprised. In the bottom of the hollow we captured two 77mm. guns, and as we moved up the rise on the other side we captured a number of machine-guns, most of them among the ruined huts near the Bihucourt-Grevillers road. Their crews were all made prisoners. Just as it began to grow light I reached the spot fixed for headquarters. On the right the 3rd and 15th Companies were now on the edge of Grevillers, and heavy machine-gun fire had commenced. As the 16th Company went over the crest between Grevillers and Biefvillers they were met with very heavy fire also. The Huns in Biefvillers woke up and opened with many machine-guns

GREVILLERS

on the 6th Company and headquarters. Here we were partially sheltered by a bank and some old iron huts, in one of which our invaluable cook started to get breakfast ready. Round this area we had captured, perhaps, a dozen machine-guns, and my runners and some of the 6th Company promptly manned them and brought them into action against Biefvillers. The brisk machine-gun duel which ensued expended much ammunition, but resulted in no casualties on either side, as far as one could judge. Later on, targets became scarcer, and, to exhibit their skill, the runners fired with impartiality at every head that appeared, without discrimination between friend and foe, so it was necessary to stop them altogether, to their manifest regret. While we were watching them fire, several tanks came in sight from the direction of Achiet-le-Petit. One of these opened fire on us with his six-pounder gun, and the rest followed suit with machine-guns, so we were now under a cross-fire from Biefvillers on the left front and the tanks on the right rear. Fortunately, no one was hit, but as the tanks advanced round Grevillers, still

GREVILLERS

firing, they caused some casualties among the men of the 3rd and 15th Companies. Round headquarters we took what cover we could, and availed ourselves of the opportunity of getting some breakfast. Presently five more tanks, of the whippet variety, came along, and the Padre and I ventured out towards them; they trained their machine-guns on us, but, fortunately, did not fire, and, going up to the nearest one, I hammered on his skin with my stick till one of the occupants emerged, and I directed them on to Biefvillers, where they did some useful work.

Meanwhile, a number of prisoners were coming out from Grevillers, and from their escorts I learned that Capt. Wood, with the 3rd Company, had cleared the village. Many of the prisoners were sent back along the road to Bihucourt, so, probably, the 37th Division got the credit for them. Presently a runner from Capt. Wood reported that Grevillers was captured, except the extreme north-eastern corner, where there were no enemy left, but where it was impossible for us to go, as the machine-gun fire was too heavy. From this

GREVILLERS

corner, where a railway siding ran into the trees, the Huns had, unfortunately, been able to remove a gun on a railway mounting with an engine attached, but in the village we had captured a battery of eight-inch howitzers. On our extreme right, after the tanks had arrived, Sergt. Forsyth, of the 15th Company, won the first Victoria Cross the Battalion had gained. This N.C.O. had joined us from the Engineers a few days previously, and showed great bravery in attacking some machine-guns. Afterwards, when a tank arrived, he walked in front of it to direct it, under heavy fire, and when the tank was disabled he organised and led its crew till he was killed by a sniper.

The Battalion had now performed its task, and reached its objective. 2/ Wellington, in support, was in touch with us, and the situation quite satisfactory. At this moment the 37th Division launched a very fine attack from Bihucourt towards Sapignies and Behagnies, which effectually cleared our left flank, though some Huns still lingered in Biefvillers till that village was finally occupied by a party from 2/ Wellington. On our right 1/

GREVILLERS

Wellington, starting their attack a little later than ours, had been equally successful, and had taken Loupart Wood.

I had received no reports from the 15th and 16th Companies, and, as time went on, became anxious to know their exact line. The 16th Company, I knew, would find it difficult to get a message back over the crest, but I thought I could get round the edge of Grevillers to them, so I started towards Grevillers with the Padre to find them. On reaching the crest, the fire from the enemy machine-guns was very heavy, and we dropped into a shell-hole to consider matters. While there I was hit in the face by the nose-cap of a small shell, and became a casualty; and as I walked out a few minutes later I met the 2nd Brigade, who were passing through us, with a view to encircling Bapaume.

The details of this successful action have been given very fully, because I consider it to have been the best piece of work the Battalion ever did. An advance of two thousand yards had been made, and a very strong position taken, without any support on either flank

GREVILLERS

or from artillery, the success being solely due to the resolution of all ranks to make good as much ground as possible for the benefit of the troops following us. We captured a number of prisoners, the exact figures being difficult to estimate, as well as many machine-guns, and a battery of eight-inch howitzers and several 77mm. guns. Our casualties in the attack and until relieved during the evening were less than eighty of all ranks, but these included seven officers, of whom Lieut. Webster was killed and Capt. Wood and Lieuts. Hewitt, Cooper, Carnahan and Peace and myself wounded. Owing to the light casualties the work done by the Battalion was not much appreciated by some who are prone to judge the difficulties encountered more by the extent of the slaughter than by the success achieved. Consequently, a murderous battle, fought on orthodox and stereotyped lines, is often considered a greater success than a less costly and more scientific encounter that has been fraught with the attainment of a definite object.

GREVILLERS

In this battle, Major McClelland and Capt. Wood handled their companies particularly well, and Lieut. Nicholls, who was acting as adjutant for the first time, carried out his duty in a most satisfactory manner.

CHAPTER X

BANCOURT

I WAS evacuated to the base the same day, and rejoined the Battalion on the 5th September. Meanwhile, important events had happened, which I can only relate from hearsay, and, therefore, do not give them the space and details which their importance deserves.

The Battalion was relieved by 1/ Auckland on the evening of the 24th August, and went into reserve, while the battalions in the front line tried to work their way round the south to the east of Bapaume, but for a day or two they were unable to cross the Albert-Bapaume road. 2/ Auckland received some reinforcements from the base, including Lieuts. Armitage and McIntyre, on the 27th, and Lieuts. Carter and Abel, on the 30th. At last the enemy was compelled, by pressure on his flanks, to abandon Bapaume, and the Division prepared to attack him to the east of the town on the morning of the 30th August.

BANCOURT

From Bapaume many main roads radiate. One of these runs nearly due east through Bancourt and Haplincourt to Bertincourt. South of this is the main road to Peronne, running through Riencourt, and north is the main road to Cambrai. The country consists of a succession of low, grassy undulations, running north and south. Bancourt is in the bottom of one such hollow, with a well-defined ridge to the east of it running from Riencourt northwards. Where the road to Bertincourt crosses this ridge there were a number of iron huts on both sides of the road. For the attack on the 30th August, 2/ Auckland was to assemble in some sunken roads near the Albert-Bapaume road, 1/ Wellington attacking on their left and the 42nd Division on their right. In my absence, Major Sinel was commanding the Battalion. The first objective was the village of Bancourt, which lay to the north-east, and, after capturing that, the Battalion was to move eastward and capture the ridge on the Bertincourt road; while the 42nd Division took Riencourt on the right

BANCOURT

and 1/ Wellington took the prolongation of the ridge to the north.

Shortly before the hour fixed for the attack, the 42nd let Major Sinel know they would not be ready to attack till later, and in accordance with orders, Major Sinel postponed his start. The result was bad. The barrage for the attack began to the north, and all the attacking force as far south as 2/ Auckland moved forward. The German artillery opened in reply, and fired very accurately on the sunken road where 2/ Auckland was assembled. One large shell burst among headquarters, slightly wounding Major Sinel and Major McClelland, who were able to remain with the Battalion, however, and severely wounding the doctor—Captain Simcox—as well as killing and wounding several others. From that time on the Padre worked the dressing station with great devotion to duty, and added not a little to his very fine record of work during the war.

When the Battalion did start, the Hun was, of course, fully alive to the attack, and it suffered heavily from machine-gun fire. Ban-

BANCOURT

court was successfully taken by the 6th Company, who were well directed by Capt. Moncrief, but much of their success was due to the vigour and courage shown by Lieut. Taylor, who deserves much of the credit for the capture of the village. The village being captured, the Battalion turned to the east, and advanced with the 16th Company on the right and the 6th Company on the left, the left of the 6th Company being on the Bertincourt road. The 42nd Division, meanwhile, had not been successful in advancing towards Riencourt, and very heavy machine-gun fire from that flank took the Battalion in enfilade. In spite of this and the fire from the front, especially from the huts on the road, the Battalion made progress and reached the ridge, but were unable to get to the top of it. They succeeded, however, in holding on to the ground won, though casualties had been heavy. That night and the following day and night very hard fighting ensued, in the course of which the Battalion improved its position, but was unable to hold the crest of the ridge. Several counter-attacks were made by the

BANCOURT

enemy, who fought in a most determined manner. In one counter-attack the Huns used two or three tanks, which caused considerable alarm, but not much damage, and, ultimately, they stuck fast and were abandoned. During the fighting the 3rd Company was sent out to cover the right flank, and they were extended over a large frontage till Riencourt was at last taken by the 42nd. On the 1st September the fighting died away, and a German retirement on the following morning was followed up by the 2nd Brigade.

Our losses in the Battalion had been very severe. More than 350 casualties were reported, and these included Lieuts. Hall, Taylor, McCreanor and Abel killed, and Lieuts. Holden, Grierson, W. Hill, Garroway, Vickerman, McIntyre, Carter and Popple wounded. Of these Lieuts. Hill and Carter died later. The officers killed were all men who had been with the Battalion for a long time, and their loss was a great blow to us.

For its share in the fighting at Grevillers and Bancourt the Battalion recéived a fair number of honours. Sergt. Forsyth won the

BANCOURT

V.C., as previously mentioned, Majors Sinel and McClelland the D.S.O., Padre Dobson, Capt. Moncrief, Lieuts. Hill, Vickerman and King the M.C., and of Military Medals there was a copious shower.

CHAPTER XI

REORGANISATION AND REST

I REJOINED the Battalion on the 5th September. They were still living on the Bancourt battlefield, and we spent the next few days in reorganising and preparing for the line again. The battle area had moved some distance to the east. On the 2nd September, when the 2nd Brigade had relieved the 1st Brigade, it was found that the enemy had gone. He was followed through Haplincourt and Bertincourt to Ruyaulcourt, where some fighting took place, and then retired further through Neuville-Bourjonval and Metz-en-Couture and Havrincourt Wood. His retreat stopped east of Metz, and he held a strong position on the high ground through the eastern edge of Gouzeaucourt Wood, Trescault and Havrincourt Village. At Havrincourt he was now back in the old Hindenburg trench system; and at first it was thought he would fall back on this also on our front to the south of that village, but, instead, he held

REORGANISATION AND REST

obstinately on to the line of African Trench. The Rifle Brigade relieved the 2nd Brigade, and on the 12th September the 1st Brigade was to relieve the Rifle Brigade. The method employed for holding this sector was for one brigade to be in the front line, one in support around Neuville, Ytres and Ruyalcourt, and one in reserve near Bancourt. The brigade in the line had three battalions in the frontline trenches and one in reserve round Metz-en-Couture, and, owing to its heavy casualties, 2/ Auckland was destined for the latter task. The distance to be moved forward was some eight miles, and was done in two stages. On the 11th we moved a short distance to a camp between Haplincourt and Bertincourt, where we spent one night; and next day we went forward again to Metz-en-Couture, where we relieved the 3/ N.Z.R.B. Meanwhile, in the early morning of the 12th September an attack had taken place, in which the Rifle Brigade had had a part. To the north the 62nd Division captured Havrincourt and Trescault villages with the front trenches of the Hindenburg Line round the former village,

REORGANISATION AND REST

while the Rifle Brigade, pivoting on its extreme right flank, kept touch with them. The operation was quite successful, except on the right of the Rifle Brigade, where our troops failed to hold a portion of their objective. The regurgitation of this fighting made the relief of the other three Rifle Brigade Battalions a somewhat difficult matter. Our own relief, however, was quite simple, and we remained here very comfortably till the 14th September. Headquarters was in a quarry just outside Metz, in the valley on the south side of the village, the 3rd Company in trenches on the spur to the east, 6th around the dump to the south, 15th in trenches to the north, and 16th in some iron huts to the south of the village. Metz-en-Couture itself was left severely alone on account of danger from shelling, the only exception being the 3rd Company Headquarters, where Major Sherson lived in a large cellar under the brewery, and was consistently shelled with gas shell every night.

The whole Division was now to be relieved by the 5th Division, and to go for a short

REORGANISATION AND REST

rest to the area round Biefvillers. We were relieved on the 14th, in the afternoon, by the 1st Royal West Kents, and marched to Villers-au-Flos, where we stayed the night. The next day we marched through Bapaume to our new home at Biefvillers, where we were to live in those huts to the north of the railway, from which we had been subjected to so much machine-gun fire in the battle of Grevillers, on the 24th August.

The fortnight we spent at Biefvillers passed very quickly and pleasantly. The men got clean clothing and baths at Bihucourt; and the Battalion did the usual training, special attention being paid to teaching Lewis gunners. Reinforcements arrived, which brought us up to strength again. We had already, while at Metz, been joined by Capt. McGregor and Lieuts. Shaw, Davenport, Hill, Mulgan, Rice, and Caughey; and with the reinforcements now received came Capt. Evans and Lieuts. Baker, Pountney, Slade, and Hanna. Capt. Evans went to command the 15th Company in place of Capt. Napier, who had gone to England a little while pre-

REORGANISATION AND REST

viously on duty, and Capt. McGregor went to the 3rd Company as second in command to Major Sherson, in succession to Capt. Wood. Davenport became Lewis gun officer; and when we left Biefvillers, and Hessall went on leave, Rice became quartermaster. On the 29th, Lieut. Crawford left for New Zealand on duty furlough, and on the 2nd October Lieut. Walker left for England, to join the Reserve Battalion.

One of the principal events of our period of rest was an inspection of the Battalion by General Russell, who seemed satisfied with the show the Battalion made. He certainly should have been; for a great deal of trouble was taken over it by everyone.

CHAPTER XII

WELSH RIDGE

WHILE we were resting some progress was made in front. Further north considerable advances had been made, and on our front east of Havrincourt Wood the Hun had been driven out of Beaucamp; and a line was now held by the 42nd Division running roughly north and south along the valley in which lies the railway from Epehy through Marcoing to Cambrai. At Marcoing this railway crosses the Escaut (or Scheldt) River, and here British troops had crossed the river and held a footing on the eastern bank. Further attacks were now contemplated, with a view to seizing the very important road and railway centre of Cambrai. Cambrai is difficult to attack from the west, as it is covered by the Escaut River. This river is canalised, and is nowhere fordable. It runs north-east from Banteux to Crêvecœur, where it turns sharply to the west through Masnieres to Marcoing, and then turns north again past the western edge of Cambrai.

WELSH RIDGE

Crêvecœur lies east of the river with a detached portion on the west bank called Rue des Vignes running in two long parallel streets along the west bank southwards. At the north end of Rue des Vignes is the Château Revelon, standing in a walled enclosure in the angle of the river. The river flows in a valley of moderate depth, with Crêvecœur lying in the valley and hidden from the west by Bonavis Ridge, which runs north and south parallel to the river. To the west of Bonavis Ridge is a wide, flat piece of ground about a mile and a half across, with the considerable village of Masnieres on the river between Crêvecœur and Marcoing at its northern edge. West of this flat again is a dry watercourse known as Vacquerie Valley, to the west of which the wide, flat-topped Welsh Ridge rises steeply and then falls again abruptly into the valley in which runs the railway from Epehy to Marcoing, which was now our front line. The 42nd Division had succeeded in pushing forward some posts across the railway and up the side of Welsh Ridge, but they did not hold the ridge.

WELSH RIDGE

The New Zealand Division was now to attack on the front held by the 42nd Division, in conjunction with attacks by other Divisions to the north and south. We were warned to be in readiness to move, and I made up our "B" teams and arranged for the companies to be commanded in the attack as follows:—

    3rd Company: Major Sherson.
    6th Company: Capt. Newton.
    15th Company: Capt. Evans.
    16th Company: Capt. Stewart.

The officers commanding the 6th and 16th Companies were thus left with the "B" team, and the seconds in command of the 3rd and 15th.

The Battalion left Biefvillers by motor lorry on the night of the 28th September, and arrived at dawn at Neuville-Bourjonval, marching thence to Ruyalcourt, where it remained for the day. It was a most unpleasant morning, with heavy showers of rain, which we had to endure in the open, as all available cover was being used by other troops.

During the morning the Brigadier had a conference at Bertincourt, and outlined the

WELSH RIDGE

scheme of operations. The plan was for the Division to attack Welsh and Bonavis Ridges, with the 2nd Brigade on the right and the 1st on the left. The 1st Brigade was to attack with 2/ Wellington on the right and 1/ Auckland on the left, these battalions being followed by 1/ Wellington and 2/ Auckland, respectively; so, instead of working with 2/ Wellington, as usual, 2/ Auckland was working with 1/ Auckland. It was anticipated that the two leading battalions would capture Welsh Ridge and get some distance further, and as soon as they stopped—probably about Bonavis Ridge—the other two battalions would pass through them and complete the operation. The final task for 2/ Auckland was to seize the crossings of the Escaut at Crêvecœur, capture Crêvecœur, and push forward posts as far as a line from the old mill of Esnes to La Targette, on the high ground the opposite side of the valley. 1/ Wellington on our right were ultimately to cross the river at Rue des Vignes, occupy Lesdain, and push forward posts to the south of 2/ Auckland. In

WELSH RIDGE

mentioning these objectives, it must not be supposed that it was expected that anyone would reach the furthest—several miles distant—on the first day, except under the most fortunate circumstances, but they were given to indicate the general line of advance, and to harmonise all movements for some distance ahead, in case of unusual success. As a matter of fact, if it had not been for the mistaken action of one battalion commander, which will be mentioned later, 2/ Auckland, at any rate, might have reached the furthest objective on the first day.

As the 42nd Division held a somewhat badly-defined line on the west side of Welsh Ridge, their posts east of the railway were to be withdrawn during the night, in order to give a clearly-defined line on which to commence the attack. The assault was to be delivered under an artillery barrage, and was timed to take place at 3.30 on the following morning; that is, it was to be a regular night attack, and two hours' darkness would follow its commencement. The 1st Brigade was to be on the march at 4.30 p.m., and move to

WELSH RIDGE

a part of the Hindenburg Line now in our hands north of Beaucamp, where we should bivouac for the night, or as much of the night as remained before our attack was delivered.

When I got back to the Battalion in the afternoon the rain had cleared off, and it remained fine all night. 2/ Auckland had the greatest distance to march, and, not wishing to be the last battalion on the road, we started as soon as possible—about 4.15 p.m.—moving along the road through Metz and Trescault with companies in column of route at 100 paces distance. Unfortunately, we were blocked by other battalions before reaching Metz, and were somewhat delayed, as most of them were marching by platoons at 50 paces distance, which took considerable time and road space. Still I hoped to reach our bivouac before 9 o'clock, and to make sure of the way I sent forward my adjutant, Capt. Tuck, through Trescault and Beaucamp, to find our place, intending that he should ride back and guide us if it became dark before we reached our destination. He misunderstood me, unfortunately, and on reach-

WELSH RIDGE

ing the place remained there. This was only the first of many misfortunes that overtook us in the next few days. As we approached Trescault and daylight was waning, I closed up our column throughout and marched without any distance between companies; not only because I consider this the best formation even close up to the front by night, but also because the road was crowded with traffic in both directions, and in this formation there is no danger of losing touch in the dark. At the same moment, however, 1/ Auckland, the battalion in front of me on the road, formed from column of platoons at 50 paces distance to column of sections at 50 paces distance, a manœuvre which made their column four times as long, taking up a distance of over two miles on a crowded road, and taking them more than half an hour to accomplish, while 2/ Auckland was kept waiting on the road in rear and losing valuable daylight. The result to 1/ Auckland was that touch was lost through their column, causing much difficulty to them later on.

WELSH RIDGE

On reaching Trescault I found the road to Beaucamp clear of troops, and turned to the right along it. A road to the left again through Beaucamp would lead me direct to our bivouac position. It was dark as we left Trescault, and, instead of turning to the left to pass through Beaucamp, I turned too soon along a track I mistook in the gloom for the road, and I soon realised I had lost my way. It was now 9 o'clock, and we had still some distance to go. By good luck we found some troops near by who gave me a guide along a short cut to Beaucamp, but it was not passable for vehicles, so we had to unload our Lewis guns from the limbers, which took more valuable time. Arriving at Beaucamp, the village appeared to be full of the 2nd Brigade, who seemed in the darkness involved in inextricable confusion, and so as not to add to it by marching through them, I waited another half hour. Finally we reached our bivouac position at 11 o'clock, and settled down for what rest we could get.

At 2.30 a.m. it was necessary for us to move forward to a position just across the

WELSH RIDGE

railway, to be in readiness for the attack. The formation of 2/ Auckland for the attack was 15th Company on the right and 16th on the left, followed, respectively, by the 3rd and 6th Companies. My orders to the company commanders of the leading companies were to keep close in touch with 1/ Auckland, and as soon as they found 1/ Auckland stopped, to pass through and make good as much ground as possible, the 3rd and 6th Companies, again, passing through the 15th and 16th when the latter were checked, so that when a check occurred there should be fresh troops behind to continue the advance. It was impossible to give any further indication of the probable position of Battalion Headquarters than a general line of advance.

When we left the bivouac area, Capt. Newton, of the 6th Company, started off too quickly, and left half his company with Lieut. Somers behind, and they followed on with Battalion Headquarters. It will be convenient to follow Capt. Newton and the half company with him first, as they fought a separate battle. Moving forward to the assembly position,

WELSH RIDGE

Capt. Newton got too far to the right, and failed to correct his error. When the attack started he got further still to the right, ending at last on the extreme right of 2/ Wellington on top of Bonavis Ridge, among the buildings south of Lateau Wood. Here his party did most valuable work, and fought a very fine action; for the 2nd Brigade, on the right, had failed to get far forward, thus leaving the right of our line exposed, except for these two platoons. Capt. Newton drove the enemy out of the buildings towards the river, but was counter-attacked in great force, and retired again to the buildings, where he held his ground. Casualties in this half compāny were heavy, and Capt. Newton was wounded, and the two subalterns with him—Mulgan and Shaw—killed.

To return to the rest of the Battalion. When the attack commenced, the 15th and 16th Companies, as arranged, followed 1/ Auckland quite closely. In the darkness and unavoidable confusion of a night attack they got into the front line, the result being that the Brigade attack went forward on a three

WELSH RIDGE

battalion front instead of two. (1/ Wellington did not get involved in the battle at all). The attack passed right over Welsh Ridge and Vacquerie Valley and across the pavé road leading south from Masnieres to the Bois Lateau, but news of the progress made did not get back to me at Battalion Headquarters, which remained at first near the railway. To keep in touch with the situation of the leading battalions I had sent my Intelligence Officer, Lieut. Eccles, with some of his men, forward with the C.O. of 1/ Auckland, so that Eccles might send word to me from time to time of the progress of events. The C.O. of 1/Auckland, however, first sent Eccles and his staff out on a patrol to bring him information, and then sent them back as escort for some prisoners. By this misuse of my men I was cut off from one principal means of keeping touch. For some time I stayed near the railway to the west of Welsh Ridge, in touch with Col. Cunningham, from whom I hoped to get information, and then moved forward to the top of the ridge. Crossing the top of the ridge with headquarters, we were met by machine-gun fire from the direct front, which was somewhat of a puzzle, but was due to some machine-gun nests on the ridge having been missed by our attack. This fire led me to think that our attack had not progressed very far, and that our front-line troops were only a little distance ahead, so I waited again here for some little time, expecting to receive messages from Eccles, which never came. Finally, as daylight just began to show, I worked round with my Headquarters to the right of the machine-gun nests, and, as it grew lighter, was able to discern some troops who seemed to be ours, in the direction of Bonavis Ridge. We moved on, therefore, down into Vacquerie Valley, working to the left, to get in rear of 2/ Auckland again. At the same time, Major Turnbull, commanding 1/ Wellington, seems to have come up against the same machine-gun nests on Welsh Ridge which I had encountered, and which were now behind us. He was proceeding to engage them, when our six-inch howitzers opened on them. This was uncomfortable for all of us. A six-inch howitzer is a dangerous weapon,

WELSH RIDGE

and their fire fell alike on the just and the unjust—the "overs" falling on me in the valley, and the "shorts" catching Major Turnbull on the ridge.

The first message from the front now came back to me, from Capt. Stewart, 16th Company, saying he was now in a position a little west of Crêvecœur, and was moving forward towards the river. We had captured several guns, many prisoners, and had lost one casualty. Numerous prisoners going back past us began also to indicate a considerable success. Expecting to find the leading companies approaching Crêvecœur, I moved forward across the flat to the pavé road to Masnieres. Here I found first Lieut. Somers with the half of the 6th Company that had not followed Capt. Newton. He told me that the advance of 2/ Auckland had been stopped by the C.O. of 1/ Auckland, who had ordered them back to this road. I could not believe it, but he directed me to the C.O. 1/ Auckland, whom I found near by, and the latter told me he had ordered my Battalion back to re-form on the pavé road. I asked him if there was anything to have prevented 2/ Auckland from reaching Crêvecœur, and he said no; but he volunteered no explanation of either his orders given to 2/ Auckland or his interference with another battalion. I asked no more, but after finding where his battalion was posted, went away, intending to stop the movement and push forward to Crêvecœur, in accordance with Brigade Orders. Close by, however, I found Major Sherson, who was already back on the road with the 3rd Company, and I saw the 15th and 16th Companies retiring in front. Considering that the withdrawal had now been completely effected, that it was broad daylight, and that all effect of surprise had gone, it seemed to me too late to renew the advance; so I reported the matter to Brigade, and returned to Vacquerie Valley, where I made my own headquarters for the rest of the day.

The extraordinary incident just mentioned, in my opinion, was the cause of robbing us of a very striking success. The failure to reach Crêvecœur, of course, was due partly to myself being out of touch with the Battalion

WELSH RIDGE

for a time, owing to the delay caused by the machine-guns on Welsh Ridge; but orders were clearly understood by the company commanders, the Battalion's casualties were negligible, three and a half companies were in a position to move, and in spite of the long advance there appears to have been little disorganisation. The two excellent officers who commanded the 15th and 16th Companies both had their companies intact, and have assured me that the advance to Crêvecœur seemed to present little difficulty, and that they were actually preparing for it when ordered back. The 3rd Company was also intact and closely supporting the 15th. My own conclusion, after thinking carefully over the matter many times, is that we might easily have captured the river crossings and Crêvecœur that day, and so have saved ourselves many casualties, besides capturing a number of Huns who escaped over the river during the morning.

To turn to the actual results of the battle. On our Divisional front we had advanced two to three miles over strongly defended country,

WELSH RIDGE

and had got well in rear of the Hindenburg defences, in addition to capturing more than a thousand prisoners and many guns. Among the spoil were three long-range guns captured by 2/ Auckland. Across the river on our left, English troops advancing from Marcoing had taken Masnieres, and, with the progress that had been made still further north, Cambrai was now half encircled.

CHAPTER XIII

CRÊVECŒUR

FOR the rest of that day, the 29th September, I left the 3rd, 15th and 16th Companies where they were, near the pavé road, but withdrew both portions of the 6th Company back to Vacquerie Valley, to enable Lieut. Somers, the only officer remaining with the Company, to make necessary reorganisation. Lieut. King, the battalion signalling officer, established telephonic communication with the other three companies to Battalion Headquarters, and from there to Brigade. The weather remained fine all day, but turned showery in the evening, and the night fell with unusual darkness. Late in the evening, Brigade sent out orders to 1/ Wellington and 2/ Auckland to continue the advance in the early morning. The idea was the same as that of the day before, namely, for 1/ Wellington, on the right, to pass through Rue des Vignes, cross the river, and move

CRÊVECŒUR

forward through Lesdain, while 2/ Auckland was to cross the river at Crêvecœur and take that village, and advance up the slopes opposite towards the old mill of Esnes. If successful, arrangements were made for a party to go in the direction of Cambrai. In the darkness, however, the runners with the orders to both battalions lost their way, and the telephone does not seem to have been thought of at that stage, even as a means of warning us that orders were on the way. At 11.15 p.m. the orders reached me by telephone, and soon after Major Turnbull came in to see me, to consult whether we should or should not have an artillery barrage, as two alternative schemes had been prepared, which gave us the option in the matter. Though we both preferred the scheme which dispensed with the barrage, we both considered it too late for certain necessary arrangements, and therefore decided on the other alternative. The attack was therefore to start under a barrage at 5.45 a.m.—just before daylight—the following morning. There was no time to waste, so we had to act independently, and,

CRÊVECŒUR

as it afterwards transpired, Major Turnbull had mistaken the time of the attack—5.45 a.m.—and thought it was 5 a.m. The order had not been clear, and I mistook the hour for 5 a.m. myself, till Capt. Tuck pointed out my mistake.

It was now 11.30 p.m., and the attack was to begin at 5.45 a.m. My plan was to concentrate the Battalion for the attack in rear of the line on which the barrage was to start by 5.30 a.m., and then to attack with the 16th Company leading, seizing the bridges and taking Crêvecœur. The 3rd Company on the right and 15th on the left were to follow, each using one platoon, or if necessary more, to assist the 16th Company in mopping up Crêvecœur; while the remaining platoons moved up the slope and pushed posts forward on to the final objective. The 6th Company was to be in reserve, and I intended to use it in exploiting success as the occasion might offer. The telephone had broken down, so I sent out a written order to the Companies by runner, and told the Company Commanders to meet me at the 15th Company Head-

CRÊVECŒUR

quarters at 2 a.m. The runners with this order lost their way also in the darkness, and it was only delivered to the 6th Company. Soon after 2 a.m., with Capt. Tuck and a runner, I reached the 15th Company Headquarters, finding it with some difficulty in the darkness, and discovered Capt. Evans asleep there, but none of the other Company Commanders. Fresh runners were sent out from the 15th Company to fetch Major Sherson and Capt. Stewart. At four o'clock these officers still had not arrived, and it was clear that it was impossible now to effect any preliminary concentration, and that companies would have to move forward independently from where they now were. Meanwhile Headquarters and the 6th Company had arrived, and were in readiness to move. It was intended that the 16th Company should lead the advance and seize Crêvecœur, as explained already, but I now decided to substitute the 15th for the 16th, as the 15th and 6th were the only companies now ready. At 4.30 a.m. Capt. Evans started forward with his company to reach the point where the barrage

CRÊVECŒUR

would begin. He had just gone when Major Sherson and Capt. Stewart arrived together, and very hurriedly I explained the operation to them. Both of these companies, the 3rd on the right and the 16th on the left, were to follow the 15th; the 3rd was to gain touch with 1/ Wellington on our right and would keep to the left of Rue des Vignes and cross the river if possible by the main bridge to Crêvecœur, and the 16th would cross by a temporary bridge which was further down stream—that is, to the left. There was no time to waste, and it was doubtful if now they were not too late to support the 15th if there was any strong opposition at the bridges.

Before continuing the narrative, it may be mentioned again that the Escaut River runs north-east past Rue des Vignes, where 1/ Wellington was to cross it, and here the map showed one permanent and two temporary bridges. At the north end of Rue des Vignes the river turns to the west, and runs due west for several miles. Just west of the bend the river is crossed by the main road to Crêvecœur by a substantial stone bridge and lock

CRÊVECŒUR

combined, and further west again, or downstream, there were two or three temporary wooden bridges. Rue des Vignes is on the slope of the valley towards the river, and the end of Bonavis Ridge running parallel to the river—that is, north and south, hides it from view. At the north end of Bonavis Ridge is the Château Revelon, in the angle of the river, entirely surrounded by a substantial brick wall. The road to Crêvecœur runs west up the ridge, on the top of which it bifurcates, the right hand branch passing the cemetery and running down to the river through Rue des Vignes to the permanent bridge; and the left hand branch skirting the wall of the Château Revelon leads over the stone bridge and lock to Crêvecœur. Turning to the left again at this bridge, and following the river bank, a roadway runs between the Château wall and the river. Crossing the bridge towards Crêvecœur, the main road turns to the left sharply along a raised bank or causeway, and then turns to the right again and crosses a second narrow but deep branch of the river by a stone bridge into the village. A

CRÊVECŒUR

second bridge crosses this smaller branch of the river further to the right. Between the two branches of the river there is an island, flat and marshy, a hundred yards wide at the east end, where the lock is situated, and narrowing to a point at the other end.

To elucidate the events which followed, it will be easier to explain first what happened to 1/ Wellington, who were supposed to attack through Rue des Vignes and cross the river on our right. As mentioned before, they had supposed 5 a.m. to be the "zero" time at which the barrage would commence. By that time they were ready to move forward, but the correct zero time was 5.45 a.m., and so no barrage began. They waited, and presently heavy artillery fire developed some distance to the right. The leading company thought that in the darkness it had got too far to the left, and immediately moved off towards the gunfire on the right, ultimately and accidentally reaching Banteux some four or five miles too far to the right. The remaining companies followed to the right, and when our barrage finally began never succeeded in reaching Rue

CRÊVECŒUR

des Vignes or in coming into action at all throughout the day.

To return now to 2/ Auckland. By 5 a.m. on the 30th September all the Company Commanders had received their orders, and the 15th Company was moving forward to be in position for the barrage. With us was a section of machine-guns, but a battery of eighteen-pounders which should also have been under my command, failed to arrive till the afternoon. About 4 a.m. the enemy had commenced counter-preparation artillery fire, and was dropping a number of shells all over our forward area in places where troops might be expected to assemble. Giving the 3rd and 16th Companies time to move, I waited till after 5 a.m., and then went forward with Headquarters and the 6th Company, going across country till we reached the road to Crêvecœur, and then moving along it till we reached the road junction on top of the hill on the west side of the river, where I made Headquarters in an old trench, while the 6th Company were behind me on the road. It was daylight now, and cold showers of rain

CRÊVECŒUR

came over. It was impossible to see anything of the fighting, and the enemy had opened fire with a 5.9 howitzer battery on the road ahead leading to Crêvecœur past the Château Revelon. This fire he kept up throughout the day.

Dealing first with the 3rd and 16th Companies, the 3rd Company on the right kept feeling to its right for 1/Wellington, who, of course, were not to be found, and reached Rue des Vignes also, just clear of the road to Crêvecœur. There were many enemy machine-guns both in Rue des Vignes and on the opposite side of the river, and these two companies proceeded to clear Rue des Vignes of Huns, sustaining some casualties in the process. Major Sherson mistook the Rue des Vignes Bridge for the bridge to Crêvecœur, and made for this point, thinking the 15th Company would have crossed here, but found the opposite bank held by the enemy.

Meanwhile the 15th Company had moved forward, as intended, and had reached the stone bridge and lock and the temporary wooden bridge two hundred yards below.

CRÊVECŒUR

They now found themselves on the Island, from which they were proceeding to cross by the bridge on their right front into Crêvecoeur, and part of the company occupied the other side of the second branch of the river. If the attack had developed as planned, its success was assured, for the enemy seemed much demoralised and was running from the buildings. Capt. Evans took up his position by the lock behind the causeway, and anxiously awaited the 3rd and 16th Companies. Presently the enemy began to show fight and counter-attacked, and, with their small numbers, the 15th was in a dangerous position. The portion across the second branch of the stream was cut off; a few were made prisoners, but most succeeded in rejoining the company, either by running the gauntlet of enemy machine-guns or waiting till darkness, when they returned in safety. The enemy casualties in this counter-attack were heavy, as they suffered severely from our Lewis gunfire, and they were unable to press their attack home. When the counter-attack commenced, Capt. Evans sent back word of

CRÊVECŒUR

the position to me, and I reinforced him with half of the 6th Company under Lieut. Somers, who was wounded as he crossed the bridge, and died next day. With Capt. Tuck I went down to the bridge to see the ground, and then returned to try to trace the 3rd and 16th Companies. When we got back, Capt. Stewart of the 16th and a sergeant of the 3rd Company came to Headquarters, both wounded, and reported where their companies were. As it was impossible to cross at Rue des Vignes, I sent orders to both companies to withdraw and collect behind Headquarters, with a view to sending them forward again through the 15th Company to Crêvecœur. The withdrawal necessarily took some time, and it was nearly midday when it was done. During the whole morning Capt. Evans had been hard pressed by the enemy, and was holding only the island, from which he found it impossible to attack Crêvecœur again by daylight, because the crossings of the small branch of the river were under accurate machine-gun fire.

I thought, however, it might still be possible to work round the left of the 15th Com-

CRÊVECŒUR

pany into the village, and sent Major Sherson to reconnoitre, with a view to taking his company over. Unfortunately, this officer was killed by a sniper, but Serg.-Major Roberts, who was with him, and in whom I had great confidence, reported against undertaking such a movement by day, and so we settled down for the rest of the day in the position we now occupied.

During the operation we lost Major Sherson and Lieut. Slade of the 16th Company, killed, and Capt. Stewart and Lieuts. Ashton, Lane, McAdam and Somers wounded, of whom Lieut. Somers died later. Major Sherson was greatly missed. His age rather unfitted him for the active duties of a Company Commander, but his sterling integrity of character and fine spirit of loyalty, as well as his stalwart courage, set a fine example. Capt. Stewart was a great loss, for as a fighting officer he perhaps had no equal in the Battalion.

The 3rd Company was now commanded for some time by Lieut. Hanna, the 6th by Sergt. Hall and later by Sergt. Bishop, till Capt.

CRÊVECŒUR

Moncrief rejoined, and the 16th by Lieut. Baker.

At Crêvecœur, Pte. Crichton gained for the Battalion its second V.C. for acts of gallantry that were particularly remarkable. Though wounded in the foot early in the action, he continued with his company (the 15th), and several times swam the small branch of the river with messages from his platoon commander to Capt. Evans. This involved also crossing a zone swept by machine-gun fire. He also, under heavy fire, removed the detonators and cut the wires connected to mines under one of the bridges.

We remained in the position occupied that day, but towards evening I placed the 16th Company in Rue des Vignes, covering all the crossings of the river on that flank, in case the enemy should attempt to return. During the day I sent out constant patrols to try to gain touch with 1/ Wellington, but was not successful in finding them. In the evening we got telephonic communication with Brigade, and were informed that next morning 1/ Auckland and 2/ Wellington would cross

CRÊVECŒUR

the river at Masnieres and attack Crêvecœur from the west; 2/ Wellington on the right, following the river, and 1/ Auckland on the left. I prepared to send out patrols into Crêvecœur to assist in clearing the town when 2/ Wellington should enter it. The attack eventuated next morning in due course, and resulted in some very severe fighting, the enemy counter-attacking in a determined manner. 2/ Wellington, however, cleared Crêvecœur, with some assistance from ourselves. 1/ Auckland sustained heavy casualties. The course of the action across the river could be watched from my headquarters, and was a most interesting spectacle; but though we could see 1/ Auckland bunched together in some of the sunken roads across the valley, we did not realise how heavily they were suffering, though it looked as if some more elastic formation would have been preferable.

After this attack the situation was unchanged till we were relieved by the Rifle Brigade on the 3rd October. We were not troubled by the enemy, except for a little spasmodic shelling of the lock and Rue des

CRÊVECŒUR

Vignes, which did us no damage. The 16th Company held the long front over a thousand yards at Rue des Vignes with three posts opposite the three bridges by which a crossing might be effected, with the remainder of the company in support in the village; while the 15th stayed on the island. The 3rd, 6th and Headquarters were on top of the hill in rear. The Engineers, of whom a party under Lieut. Thomas was with us, built a foot-bridge across the main stream to the island beside the lock just on the water level. This bridge was ingeniously constructed, and had a width of three planks, except at the most critical point, where it passed round one of the piers of the lock, and its width was reduced to one plank only. At this point much caution was necessary, and even with that on a dark night someone was sure to tumble into the river. Many of the Rifle Brigade did so on the night when they relieved us, but I believe all were fished out again. The houses near this place were full of German stores of all descriptions, flares, ammunition, detonators and similar material, the area round Crêvecœur having

CRÊVECŒUR

apparently been extensively used as a dump. Close to the bridge we captured among other things two medium minenwerfer.

For their work in the battle, Capt. Evans received a bar to his Military Cross, Lieut. Lang the Military Cross, and Sergt.-Major Evans the D.C.M. A number of Military Medals were also awarded.

On the 3rd October 2/ Auckland was relieved by the 4/ N.Z.R.B., and moved to the neighbourhood of Vacquerie Valley, where we lived comfortably in the old dugouts of the Hindenburg Line during two or three wet days. Reinforcements arrived, and we were joined on the 5th October by Lieuts. Brackenridge and Maynard, on the 7th by Lieut. Gordon, and on the 8th by Lieuts. Claridge, Closey, Sage and Mills. We spent the time in reorganisation and training Lewis gunners.

CHAPTER XIV

FONTAINE-AU-TERTRE FARM

THE next advance took us forward a considerable distance, and it is necessary to describe the ground we passed over. From Hébuterne to Crêvecœur we had been traversing country devastated by the Huns before their retreat in 1917. Every village, even every house, had been systematically destroyed. The limit of this area of destruction on our front was marked by the Escaut River, and Crêvecœur was intact, except for damage from shell fire alone. The towns in front of us were not only undamaged, but still retained their civilian population, though many of the inhabitants were evacuated to areas farther back as we advanced.

From the valley of the Escaut at Crêvecœur the ground rises to the road from Cambrai to Esnes, which runs along the top if the hills on the north side of the valley. Esnes itself lies in a small valley formed by

FONTAINE-AU-TERTRE FARM

the Torrent d'Esnes, which joins the Escaut at Crêvecœur. East of the Escaut, with its western edge roughly marked by the Cambrai-Esnes road, is a wide plateau, extending for some distance at a high level and unmarked by any special natural features. On this plateau are the manufacturing towns of Ligny, Caudry and Beauvois, the last-named forming one town with Fontaine-au-Pire. The roads and railways from Cambrai radiate over this plateau, the main road to Le Cateau passing Beauvois and Caudry. This plateau is some ten miles in width, and falls on its eastern side into the valley of the Selle River, which flows through Le Cateau, Briastre, Solesmes and St. Python towards the north, ultimately joining the Escaut River near Valenciennes. It is interesting to note that at the battle of Le Cateau, in 1914, the British left wing held a line running from Le Cateau through Caudry to Esnes.

On the 8th October the attack on the German positions flanking Cambrai was renewed. The Rifle Brigade advanced from Crêvecœur up the spur between the Escaut River and the

FONTAINE-AU-TERTRE FARM

Torrent d'Esnes, by a daylight attack, in which they made extensive use of a smoke barrage of rifle bombs against the Hun machine-guns. The attack was well executed against a strong position, and they reached the line of the Esnes-Cambrai road between the old mill of Esnes and Seranvillers. The Huns began to fall back, and at last abandoned Cambrai, and they were followed on our front by the 2nd Brigade, who advanced through Fontain-au-Pire and Beauvois and across the Le Cateau-Cambrai road.

On the 9th October we were ordered to move, and we started in the morning, lunching on the road near Crêvecœur, and continuing forward in the afternoon past Esnes up the hill to our bivouac position east of Longsart, near the old mill of Esnes. Brigade Headquarters was at Longsart. For the night we "dug in" in a cutting and made headquarters in a wayside shrine. During the night we were shelled intermittently by a long-range gun, which did us no damage, but caused several casualties to the Vickers gunners near us. Next morning, the 10th

FONTAINE-AU-TERTRE FARM

October, there was a conference at Brigade Headquarters, when the position was explained and orders outlined for passing the 1st Brigade through the 2nd Brigade to the line of the Selle River. It appeared that the 2nd Brigade had crossed the Le Cateau-Cambrai road between Beauvois and Caudry, and was slowly pushing back the Hun rearguards. An Otago battalion astride the Caudry-Briastre road was approaching Viesly. 2/ Canterbury on the left was not quite so far forward, and was about Aulicourt and Herpigny farms, with its right in touch with Otago and its left in touch with the Guards Division between Bevillers and Quievy. The 1st Brigade was now to pass through and relieve the 2nd Brigade, with 1/ Wellington on the right and 2/ Auckland on the left, and advance during the night to the line of the Selle River. 1/ Wellington would pass through Viesly and reach the river at Briastre, and 2/ Auckland would reach it between Briastre and the edge of Solesmes. The advance had not gone so far on the left as on the right. The Division on our right was well

FONTAINE-AU-TERTRE FARM

forward, and the Guards on the left not quite up to us. Beyond—that is east of—Aulicourt and Herpigny farms is a hollow in which was a light railway from Quievy to Bethencourt; then the ground rises again and falls farther east to another hollow in which was a second light railway from Quievy to Viesly; then rises again to a ridge running from Viesly northwards to Fontaine-au-Tertre Farm; and then falls first gradually and later more steeply into the deep valley of the Selle River, some three thousand yards east of Fontaine-au-Tertre Farm. Our line of advance just included Fontaine-au-Tertre Farm on our left. At the farm there is an important road junction from which roads radiate to Quievy, Viesly, Briastre and Solesmes.

I decided to advance with the 3rd Company on the right and the 6th on the left, both of which companies were to reach the Selle River. The 15th Company in support would establish itself on a line along the top of the high ground between Viesly and Fontaine-au-Tertre Farm, and the 16th would be in reserve

FONTAINE-AU-TERTRE FARM

near Headquarters. As the operation would be done in darkness, all movements had to be made by compass bearing. It was obvious that unless the Guards advanced considerably the left flank was exposed, so the section of the Wellington Machine Gun Company attached to 2/ Auckland was ordered by me to cover the left from the neighbourhood of Fontaine-au-Tertre. A section of eighteen-pounders was also to be attached to 2/ Auckland for the occasion. The whole manœuvre was in the nature of an advanced guard action, and I thought it best to finish with the Battalion disposed in considerable depth; and on this account I felt sure all the Company Commanders considered my dispositions quite wrong. In the advance 2/ Wellington was to follow and support 2/ Auckland, and 1/ Wellington would be supported by 1/ Auckland.

We had a long distance to cover, and so started at 2 o'clock for a point across the Le Cateau-Cambrai road near Beauvois, where the Battalion halted for its evening meal. To this point the Battalion was led by Capt. Evans, while I rode through Fontain-au-Pire

FONTAINE-AU-TERTRE FARM

and Beauvois to pass 2nd Brigade Headquarters, and so glean the latest news of the advance. I learnt that Lieut.-Col. Stewart, of 2/ Canterbury, had his headquarters at Aulicourt Farm, and decided to head for that point in the first place.

During the retrograde movement the Huns were now commencing, they destroyed all communications as much as possible. On the railways they did this by blowing up all the culverts and bridges, and causing large craters in the track by land mines. They blew up some of these mines before retiring, and fitted others with delay action contrivances, which caused them to explode at intervals during the next few weeks, and so greatly interrupt our supplies. In the same way culverts and bridges were blown up on the roads, and craters caused by mines at points where the traffic would be considerable or in cuttings and other places where it would be difficult to make a road to avoid the point. I saw one such crater in Fontaine, into which a six-inch gun had fallen, and there were many others in all the area we were now to pass through.

FONTAINE-AU-TERTRE FARM

The Battalion reached the pre-arranged place and had tea before darkness set in. At this place we left the transport. Rations for next day had not arrived, and I decided to keep the 16th Company even further back than I had intended, to carry them up later on, if possible. In the darkness we reached Aulicourt Farm, where I found Lieut.-Col. Stewart, and I decided to keep Headquarters here for some time, sending the 16th to Herpigny Farm, while the rest of the Battalion was continuing the advance. I found here, also, the section officer of the eighteen-pounders to be attached to 2/Auckland, and arranged for him to be at Fontaine-au-Tertre Farm with his guns at 4 a.m. next morning. Rations arrived while we were here, and also an order from Brigade to continue the advance, if no strong opposition was met with, across the Selle River and to the railway cutting on the hill on the further side. This order was passed on to companies, the only ones it affected being the 3rd and 6th, as it did not seem advisable for the 15th to move further. During the night the advance con-

FONTAINE-AU-TERTRE FARM

tinued steadily, and met with little opposition, as the Huns fell back as soon as contact was gained at any point, and in the early morning the 3rd and 6th reached the Selle River. The Huns had blown up the railway bridge over the river at Solesmes, and the débris blocked the river, causing the water to rise so considerably that it was impossible to effect a crossing, and we were only able therefore to establish posts on the line of the river. On our right, at Briastre, 1/ Wellington found a bridge intact, and were able to get a company over to the other side. I reached Fontaine Farm between 4 and 5 o'clock in the morning, having left the 16th Company and Headquarters some little distance behind. Later they were sent for and established in the bank of the road from Fontaine-au-Tertre Farm to Viesly. As it grew light some movement was reported on our left front, and from near the farm we were able to see distinctly large parties of men moving about some two or three thousand yards away in the direction of St. Python. At first we could not distinguish who they were, but they proved to be Huns; and as we

FONTAINE-AU-TERTRE FARM

watched they seemed to be forming into two waves, facing our exposed left flank and apparently preparing for an attack. They made the finest target for artillery I have seen, but our eighteen-pounder section, due to arrive at this very spot at 4 a.m., had not materialised, and did not appear till nearly 9 a.m., and so missed an unusual opportunity. On this flank the 15th Company was in touch with a company of the Guards at the farm, but the 6th was now nearly three thousand yards ahead on the Selle River. The Vickers guns were posted on this flank, however, and prevented any counter-attack developing against us. About 8 o'clock in the morning the Guards advanced on our flank. As an attack their movement was a failure, and fizzled out near the farm, but it provided a sufficient number of troops on that flank to relieve us of much anxiety.

In the advance we had lost one casualty only, Sergt.-Major Evans, of the 15th Company. During the morning we were unlucky in losing a number of casualties in the 3rd Company from a sudden burst of shelling on

FONTAINE-AU-TERTRE FARM

a point where a number of them were concentrated in a hollow near the river, and that evening several men on a ration party were wounded.

The R.A.P. had been established in Fontain-au-Tertre Farm, which was shelled heavily by the Huns throughout the day. The doctor and his staff were unhurt, but must have viewed the walls crumbling around them with some apprehension. In the evening the doctor moved to near Viesly, because the stretcher-bearers would not go near the farm.

The next day passed off quietly, and on the evening of the 12th we were relieved by the 42nd Division, and moved back to billets at Fontaine-au-Pire.

CHAPTER XV

RESTING AT FONTAINE AND SOLESMES

THE rest we now had for the next week at Fontaine-au-Pire was a very pleasant holiday. For the first time for six months we were living in real houses, made comfortable for billets during the Hun occupation. The whole Division was concentrated in Beauvois and Fontaine, and we were able to see something of the other battalions. These places had been used by the Huns for a veterinary hospital, and they had accumulated stores that were very useful to us. There was, for instance, in the building we used for the Quartermaster's store a large stock of coal, and though the weather was colder we were able to keep ourselves warm and dry. Only mild training was gone in for. Perhaps the most interesting occurrence was a visit from the Prince of Wales on the 14th October. 2/ Auckland was assembled with the rest of the Brigade on the road west of Fontaine, and

RESTING AT FONTAINE AND SOLESMES

cheered the Prince as he rode past—with the usual gruesome effect which organised efforts at spontaneity produce.

On the 15th October Capt. McFarland rejoined the Battalion, after a long absence, due to the wound he received at La Signy Farm; and Lieuts. Anderson, Warren, Gardner and Munro also joined. On the 9th Lieut. Caughey had been evacuated sick, and Lieut. Armitage was evacuated on the 15th. Capt. McFarland now commanded the 16th Company again. On the 17th October Lieut. Hill relieved Lieut. Raymond as transport officer; the latter officer had done extraordinarily good work throughout the summer, and was now anxious to return to his company.

Before we left Fontaine we were joined by the Bishop of Nelson, who remained with the Battalion for a fortnight, and he seemed to enjoy the experience as much as we appreciated his company.

Meanwhile the Hun was still holding a strong line along the high ground on the east side of the Selle River. An attack along the line of the river was made on the 24th Octo-

RESTING AT FONTAINE AND SOLESMES

ber, and he was driven from his position on our old front by the 42nd Division, and from Solesmes by the 62nd. Our 2nd Brigade passed through the 42nd Division and continued a most successful advance, to understand which some further description of the ground is necessary.

East of the Selle River is a plateau falling gradually to north. Its highest portion, between the Sambre River and the road from Le Cateau to Bavai, is covered by the great Foret de Mormal, of which large portions had been cut down for timber by the Germans. In bygone days this forest was of vast extent, and spread far to the north; and even now all the country east of the Selle River as far as Mons, and north as far as Valenciennes, bears traces of the forest in the scattered woods that are its remnants. Numerous small tributaries of the Escaut River take their rise in the forest, and flow north-west in deep valleys through the plateau. These, taken in order from the Selle River eastwards, are the Harpies, flowing through Vendigies, Vertigneul and Romeries; the St. Georges, flowing through Salesches,

RESTING AT FONTAINE AND SOLESMES

past Pont à Pierre Farm and through Escarmain and Bermerain; and the Ecaillon, flowing through Louvignies, Ghissignies and Beaudignies. None of these streams are formidable obstacles in themselves, but the valleys through which they run give a succession of defensive positions to a retiring army.

Beyond the Ecaillon River, on top of the plateau, is the old town of Le Quesnoy. This town is surrounded by a double rampart with a moat between, and the moat can be flooded from a small stream. The fortifications were designed by Vauban in ancient times; and its position then was of some importance, since it lies midway between the Sambre and Escaut Rivers, in the gap through which an invasion of France from the north-east is most easily possible. Beyond Le Quesnoy again is the Rhonelle River, running through Villereau and Orsinval. The main road from Solesmes to Bavai passes through Romeries, Pont à Pierre, Beaudignies and Le Quesnoy, crossing all the valleys at right angles.

On the 24th October the 2nd Brigade, passing through the 42nd Division on the high

RESTING AT FONTAINE AND SOLESMES

ground east of the Selle River, made a remarkable advance of some six miles; crossing the Harpies, St. George and Ecaillon rivers, and establishing itself on the high ground between Beaudignies and Le Quesnoy. On their left, other troops carried the advance forward, and prolonged the line towards Valenciennes, but on the right the advance continued only to the edge of the Foret de Mormal. The Rifle Brigade followed them in support, and the 1st Brigade moved to Solesmes, where Divisional Headquarters was established the same day. 2/Auckland marched to Solesmes through Bevillers and Quievy.

It was expected that the advance would be continued immediately, but this was prevented by force of circumstances. The main reason for the delay was the inability of the supply service to keep pace with any further advance. Railway communication over the wide area across which we had advanced was maintained with great difficulty. All lines had to be newly laid, and the material for them brought up along communications already congested with troops, ammunition and sup-

RESTING AT FONTAINE AND SOLESMES

plies of all sorts. When the railway was re-laid the troubles of the engineers were not ended, because the cunningly-hidden mines which the Huns had left behind could not all be discovered; and from time to time these blew new gaps in the line in the most inconvenient places. With these difficulties to contend with and overcome, it was impossible to move forward; although the advance of the 2nd Brigade had shown that the enemy was now incapable of making a stand. The problem was now not one of fighting, but one of transport.

2/ Auckland remained at Solesmes accordingly, till the 3rd November. The weather was good, and the billets not uncomfortable, though the town had been considerably damaged by the violent shelling it received from the Huns after they had been driven out. Solesmes was full of French civilians, whom the Huns had not had time to remove according to their usual policy when leaving. Their chief idea seemed to be to take all the civil population with them on their retreat, in order to get the benefit of the rations issued by the

RESTING AT FONTAINE AND SOLESMES

Relief Commission; for in the occupied districts this commission still carried on the work commenced by the Americans in the early days of the war.

We were able to do some training at Solesmes, and reconnaissances forward through Beaudignies towards Le Quesnoy were made by myself and the Company Commanders. Meanwhile, further reinforcements had joined the battalion, among whom were Lieuts. Murdoch, Knott, Des Forges, Quelch and Macdonald. Lieut. Hanna was evacuated sick, and Lieut. Clapham proceeded to England on duty. On the 3rd November I went on leave, and was away till the 20th November, so that I unfortunately missed the battle of Le Quesnoy, which turned out to be the final battle of the war.

CHAPTER XVI

LE QUESNOY

MAJOR SINEL came from the "B" team to command 2/ Auckland in the battle. The part played by the Battalion in the battle was a very minor one, as, for the first time in its history, the Battalion was in reserve.

The plan of attack for the Division was for the 1st and 3rd Brigades to surround Le Quesnoy, and for the 2nd Brigade to pass through them and continue the advance through the Foret de Mormal. The 1st Brigade was to assemble by the Ecaillon River north of Beaudignies, and in the early morning of the 4th November move to a position just across the railway north of Le Quesnoy. From this point it would attack with 1/ Auckland on the right and 2/ Wellington on the left, moving towards the forest. 1/ Auckland, pivoting on its right flank, would change front towards the south, ultimately getting in touch with the Rifle Brigade east of Le Ques-

LE QUESNOY

noy, and so completely investing that town. The advance would be continued to the edge of the forest by the two Wellington battalions, 2/Auckland remaining in reserve all the time. From the edge of the forest the advance was to be continued by the 2nd Brigade.

Following out this plan, on the afternoon of the 3rd November 2/Auckland, with the rest of the Brigade, moved from Solesmes to its bivouac position near Beaudignies. The march was tiresome, owing to repeated checks caused by congestion of traffic on the roads. Next morning in darkness the Brigade moved to its preliminary position north of Le Quesnoy, 2/Auckland being in a sunken road, where it remained for some time. The attack was delivered before daylight, and went off exactly as planned. Le Quesnoy was surrounded and its garrison captured. The Huns failed to make any stand, and those who were not captured fled, and the pursuit was carried on through the forest by the 2nd Brigade. 2/Auckland moved to Villereau, and the only work done by the Battalion was to place posts in the forest covering the left flank of the

LE QUESNOY

advance, for which purpose the 16th Company was employed.

The Division was relieved by the 42nd Division, and 2/Auckland returned through Solesmes to Beauvois, which was reached on the 11th November, the day of the Armistice.

CHAPTER XVII

THE ARMISTICE

AFTER the Armistice the whole Division was concentrated in and around Beauvois, and preparations were soon commenced for a long march, which would bring it to a point where it would entrain for Cologne, near which place we were destined to be one of the divisions to occupy the bridgehead zone across the Rhine. The prospect was welcomed by almost all, but there were a few grumblers, as usual, who did not want the march. We spent the time in getting ready to move. Route marching by Brigades was practised a good deal, and ceremonial drill; and General Russell inspected the transport of every unit. The weather became much colder, and two blankets were issued to each man.

A good many changes took place among the officers of the Battalion. Capt. McGregor left for England on the 8th November, Major McClelland had gone on extended leave on

THE ARMISTICE

the 3rd, and on the 11th Major Sinel went to take command of the Reserve Battalion of the Auckland Regiment at Sling. By these changes Capt. Evans became the next senior officer to myself in the Battalion, and carried out the duties of Second in Command during all the last phase of our existence. He was exceptionally well qualified for the work, and carried it out in a most able and satisfactory manner. A number of officers received temparary rank to fill the vacancies which now existed, and the following table shows the respective company commanders and seconds in command of companies during the rest of the year:—

3rd Company—
    O.C.: Lieut. (t.-Capt.) Hessall.
    2nd i/c.: Lieut. (t.-Capt.) Warren.

6th Company—
    O.C.: Lieut. (t.-Capt.) Moncrief, M.C.
    2nd i/c.: Lieut. (t.-Capt.) Speer.

15th Company—
    O.C.: Capt. Macdonald.
    2nd i/c.; Lieut. (t.-Capt.) Pountney.

THE ARMISTICE

16th Company—
    O.C.: Capt. (t.-Major) McFarland, M.C.
    2nd i/c.: Lieut. (t.-Capt.) Baker.

The Battalion Staff was composed as follows:—
    C.O.: Lieut.-Col. S. S. Allen, D.S.O.
    2nd i/c.: Capt. (t.-Major) Evans, M.C.
    Adjutant: Lieut. (t.-Capt.) Tuck, M.C.
    Quartermaster: Lieut. Rice, M.M.
    Asst.-Adjutant: Lieut. Nicholls.
    Signalling Officer: Lieut. King, M.C.
    Lewis Gun Officer: Lieut. Sage, M.M.
    Transport Officer: Lieut. L. J. Hill.
    Intelligence Officer: Lieut. Eccles.

Later, Lieut. Nicholls became Education Officer, Lieut. Sage Assistant Adjutant, and Lieut. Vickerman, M.C., Lewis Gun Officer.

We were joined by more reinforcements, which included the following officers, some of whom were rejoining:—Lieuts. Ramsey, Goulding, Moss, Earl, Gunn, Vickerman, J. L. Hill, Hewitt and Caughey. On the 25th November Lieut. Gordon was evacuated sick.

THE ARMISTICE

For the march we were allotted one motor lorry and one G.S. wagon for carrying blankets, in addition to the two ordinary baggage wagons; and when the time came to move 2/Auckland was the only battalion in the Brigade not compelled to abandon a certain quantity of stores. This was due to the care that had been taken by us to dispense with surplus kit and baggage of all kinds, and to remain completely mobile.

It was rumoured before we started that the march would be to Charleroi only, where we expected to entrain, but finally we marched right through Belgium; and few of those who did the journey will ever regret it. From all points of view we were well repaid for the somewhat arduous travelling of the next four weeks.

CHAPTER XVIII

THE MARCH THROUGH BELGIUM

THE march commenced on the 29th November. 2/ Auckland started before 7 o'clock in the morning and reached its billets at Bermerain by 12.30 p.m., after a march of nearly fourteen miles. The acting-brigadier allowed us no lunch halt, which made the march unnecessarily strenuous, and caused us to have no less than twenty men fall out on the way. This was the only day on which there were any stragglers from 2/ Auckland at all. During all the rest of the journey we never had a single man fall out from the Battalion, a record which constitutes no little accomplishment, and speaks volumes for the *"esprit de corps"* of the Battalion. Bermerain was an ordinary French village, somewhat damaged during the fighting, but we were not uncomfortable for the night.

On the 30th we marched to Wargnies-le-Petit. The direct road was reported impassable, so the route taken was through Maresches. On this and every subsequent

THE MARCH THROUGH BELGIUM

march of any length a halt was made of one hour for lunch. At Wargnies-le-Petit almost the whole Battalion was billeted in a very large château, which had been used by the Huns for a hospital. The panelling on the walls, bannisters, and every piece of woodwork that could be moved had been stripped from it—probably for firewood—and only the bare walls and floors were left.

Next day we marched to Bavai, where most of the battalion was accommodated in the buildings of the railway station and factory near by. A halt of one day was made here, and the doctor and chiropodist became busily employed with the lame.

We resumed our journey on the 3rd December, marching to Louvroil, a suburb of Maubeuge, on the banks of the Sambre River. The day was wet, and the march, in consequence, was far from pleasant till the afternoon, when the weather slightly improved. Maubeuge is an interesting old town, surrounded by ancient ramparts and a girdle of more modern forts; and in 1914 it had held out for several days against the Huns,

THE MARCH THROUGH BELGIUM

after the retreat from Mons had commenced. Our army, retreating from Mons, and threatened with the envelopement of its left wing, had narrowly escaped being driven into Maubeuge and surrounded.

Next day we marched to Jeumont over the rather poor roads which fringe the border of France and Belgium, and here we were again on the banks of the Sambre, the valley of which we followed fairly closely as far as Namur, where it joins the Meuse.

The following day, the 5th December, we crossed the border into Belgium, and had a rather long march to Lobbes, ending with a very stiff hill out of the valley. Our first billets in Belgium were at Lobbes, and we were most hospitably treated by the natives, of whose kindness here and throughout the whole march through Belgium it is impossible to speak too highly. All ranks were treated with the same kindness, and all the inhabitants seemed to vie with one another in their endeavour to make some return for the debt which Belgium undoubtedly owes to England and the Colonies.

THE MARCH THROUGH BELGIUM

We had a day's rest at Lobbes, and on the 7th marched to Marchiennes, a suburb to the west of Charleroi. Billets here were very scattered, and we were worse off than in any other place on the march. Everyone went in to Charleroi in the afternoon to see the city, which is the centre of the Belgian coalfields. Major Evans and I had the best tea in Charleroi we had had for a long time, consisting of creamy "gateaux" of the kind which since the days of rationing began had long been extinct in England. Here, though the prices were enormous, it was possible to buy almost anything.

On the 8th December we marched to Moignelée, a small village just big enough to contain the Battalion most comfortably. It was the day of the annual fête of the village— the local Saint's day. In the afternoon the natives played a peculiar kind of ball game, but our bands proved too strong a counter-attraction; and in the evening there was a dance, which the troops seemed to enjoy. The rest of the Brigade was in the adjacent village of Tamines, in which in 1914 the Huns had shot five hundred civilians against a wall in cold blood.

On the 9th we marched to Moustier, where we were again comfortably housed, and we had another rest for one day. Moustier is a little town, with just sufficient accommodation for one battalion, and has a local glass-making industry. This had been stopped during the Hun occupation, and our transport was now billeted in the glass factory.

The 11th December was one of our worst experiences on the march. The day was cold, with frequent storms of rain, and when we arrived at Emines in the middle of a heavy shower we found the billeting officer had only got accommodation enough for half the Battalion. After some delay, however, we were able to find room for two companies and the transport in the village of St. Mark, three kilometres away. One of the forts which form a ring round Namur is near Emines. It had been destroyed by the Huns and everything of value removed, but it was still interesting to examine. In the afternoon I rode into Namur with Major Evans, to look at the town, which

THE MARCH THROUGH BELGIUM

is situated at the junction of the Sambre and Meuse Rivers.

Next day we marched to Landenne, where we were billeted with some difficulty in a small village. On the way, not far from Emines, we passed three Zeppelin sheds; their size and construction was very remarkable.

From Landenne we marched to Huy on the 13th December, and stayed there till the 17th, to give everyone a bath and a change of clothing, which was much needed by this time, and to enable damaged boots to be mended or replaced. The hard marching had caused much wear to our boots, which badly needed attention. Everyone enjoyed the holiday at Huy, though there is not much to see in the town. It is situated in the valley of the Meuse, on both sides of the river, about half way between Namur and Liege. On the east bank is the old citadel, which was an attraction to most people. Others preferred the material pleasures of the Huy shops, and twice every day the Padre and Eccles each ate a dozen fresh pastry cakes, sitting in the shop,

THE MARCH THROUGH BELGIUM

so as to catch them coming hot from the oven. Some of the officers went over the Sugar Factory, said to be the largest in the world, to which the syrup is pumped through long pipelines from subsidiary factories as far as sixty kilometres distant.

Our rest came to an end on the 17th December, and we marched to Jemeppes—a distance of fifteen miles. I sent Capt. Moncrief and about seventy men by river steamer from Huy to Jemeppe. The whole of the route was along the Meuse Valley; at Jemeppe we were within a mile or two of Liege, and many went in by tram to see the town.

The next day was one of the worst days we had on the march, with very cold rain driving from the north-east. We did not have far to go, crossing the river and climbing up from the valley to Embourg. We were not comfortably billeted, and the 15th Company was two miles in rear of the 6th and 16th, who were in Fort d'Embourg. The fort is one of the celebrated ring of forts round Liege. It had been partially dismantled, but we could

THE MARCH THROUGH BELGIUM

find no trace of it ever having been bombarded, except a few marks that had possibly been caused by shrapnel. It seemed evident that the fort had been surrendered in 1914 without much resistance, and it was obvious throughout this district that little had been done at that time to delay the enemy's advance by destroying road and railway communication.

On the morning of the 19th we had to make an early start. We were in rear of the rest of the Brigade, and had a long distance to march, the 15th Company having to cover a distance of no less than eighteen and a-half miles. Our destination was Verviers, the last large town in Belgium. No one who was on that day's march will ever forget it. The weather was perfect for marching, fine, clear and cold; and during the morning we marched over the hills towards Pepinster. At a point on top of the hills, after marching through a forest, we came out in a clearing, from which there was a magnificent view across the valley to the south-east towards Spa. After lunch we descended into a valley at Pepinster, and

THE MARCH THROUGH BELGIUM

followed the course of a small river along to Verviers, which we reached at 4 o'clock. Here we were received with greater enthusiasm than at any other place on the march. The whole population of the town had turned out to welcome us, and treated us with the utmost kindness and hospitality.

Our last march in Belgium was on the following day, the 20th December, when we marched from Verviers in the afternoon up the valley and across a hill to Herbesthal, just across the border in Germany, setting foot on German soil for the first time. The night was bitterly cold, with showers of driving sleet. We entrained at Herbesthal during the night, and, getting what sleep we could on the train, reached Ehrenfeld, a suburb of Cologne, at 9 o'clock on the morning of the 21st.

We detrained at Ehrenfeld and marched off through Cologne at 10 o'clock. The Y.M.C.A. provided every one with a cup of tea and some biscuits, both when getting on to and leaving the train, so I did not halt for breakfast till 11 o'clock, when we were in the middle of the town, and we provided an

THE MARCH THROUGH BELGIUM

interesting spectacle for the Huns who watched us having our meal. We crossed the bridge of boats to Mulheim, and continued on a long dreary march over the dismal country through Wiesdorf and Opladen. At Opladen we halted for tea just before darkness came on, and soon after reached our destination at Berg Neukirchen.

At Berg Neukirchen this record must end. Demobilisation commenced forthwith, and the Battalion rapidly melted away.

CHAPTER XIX

THE END

TO break with old associations is always sad, and no one who was long with 2/ Auckland could leave the Battalion without some feeling of regret. 2/ Auckland was always a happy family, and all ranks worked together with the greatest harmony. In the bald record of this narrative it has been impossible to describe individual actions, except in a few striking cases; and, indeed, it would be unfair to do so when the same spirit actuated every man, and it was only the opportunity to obtain distinction that was sometimes lacking. Officers, non-commissioned officers and men all showed the same unselfishness, self-sacrifice and courage.

I cannot offer any adequate tribute to the loyalty and help of all ranks to myself as their Commanding Officer. No one could wish for finer men to fight with, or for more wholehearted support than I received.

THE END

In the foregoing pages no criticism has been made of any military operations, and the facts only have been set out as fairly and accurately as it has been possible. Some such operations are sure to be more successful than others; but the final success and the high reputation which the Division earned proved the skill with which it was handled; and the same may be said of the various units within the Division. Mention has been made of certain cases where the movements of troops did not accurately coincide, and of one case at least in which my own opinion was sharply in conflict with that of another officer. In fighting such as we did during the year, when large masses of troops were being manœuvred, it is impossible for perfect timing to be secured in the movement of units; and it is equally so for all commanding officers to look at a situation from the same point of view. Circumstances arise which prevent absolute co-ordination, and the fact that in some instances other units did not move when we did, or failed to reach their objective, must not be considered to reflect adversely on the ability

THE END

with which they were handled. If mistakes were sometimes made by others, they occurred in 2/ Auckland occasionally also.

There is nothing more to add. I hope that this book will help to remind those who served in 2/ Auckland of the great events in which they were engaged, and to sustain their interest in those who served with them. Though the time through which we have passed together has been strenuous, and many of its incidents painful, yet the memory of those who were with us will always be pleasant, and there are many happy recollections of which we shall always like to be reminded.

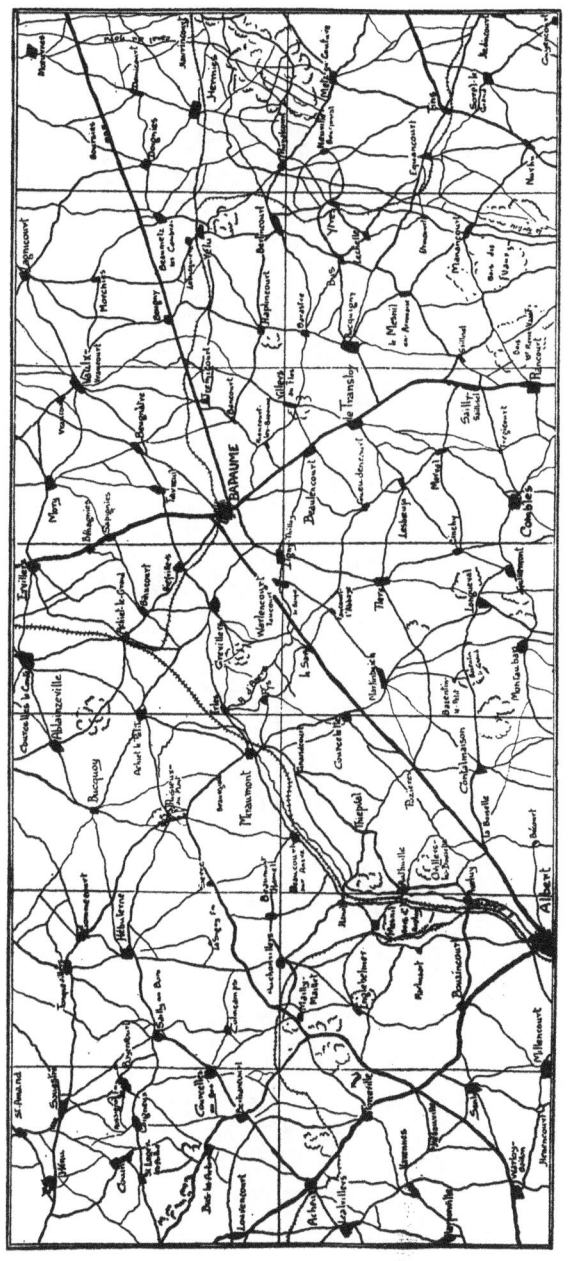

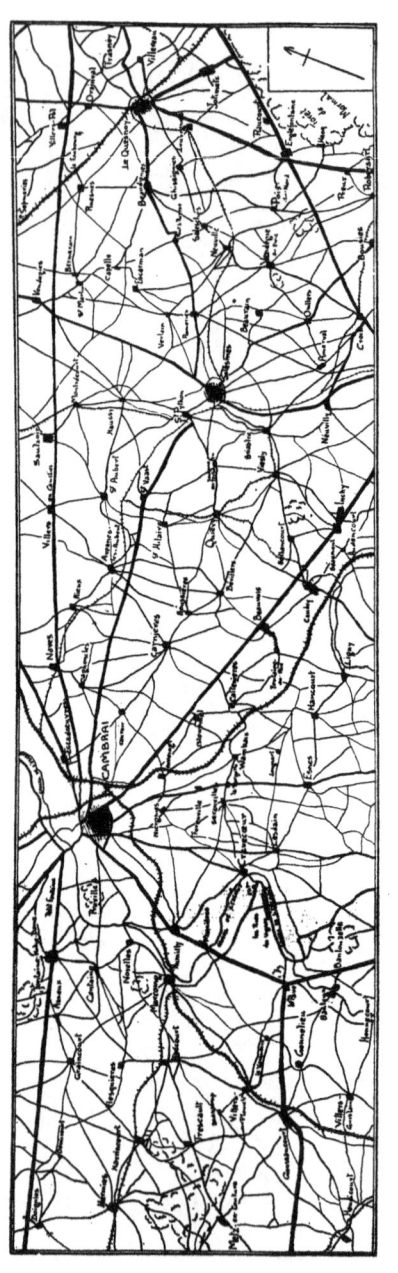

www.ingramcontent.com/pod-product-compliance
Lightning Source LLC
Chambersburg PA
CBHW031955080426
42735CB00007B/399